Stellar Leadership: Igniting Excellence Beyond the C-Suite

Elevate, Empower, and Transform the Future of Executive Influence
Galactic Command: Mastering Executive Leadership for a
New Era of Influence and Impact

Dr. Avis D. Dickey

Paperback ISBN: 978-1-971045-27-

Published by:

Pire Book Writing

www.PineBookWriting.com

R-10225 Yonge St Suite #250, Richmond Hill, ON L4C 3B2,
Canada.

Printed in the United States of America

For my mother
an educator whose joy and love of learning
inspired others to grow,
and who showed that leadership begins with
love.

Foreword

Writing this book led me to reflect on the highlights, challenges, and even the missteps I witnessed in executive leadership. My approach has always centered on "us" and "we"—how we can collectively advance for the greater good—rather than on individual achievement. True leadership, especially when it's about empowering others, means setting aside personal interests and doing what benefits everyone.

My own path in leadership has held both rewards and difficulties, requiring self-belief, vision, and revisiting plans as necessary. In leadership, as in life, learning is continuous: you must always strive to reach further, to bring others along, and to make a tangible difference. I've grown from the examples of supportive leaders, both within my experience and from a global viewpoint.

Yet, in probing deeper, I have come to realize that leadership is not merely a title or a milestone—it is an ongoing journey of humility, curiosity, and courage. The world of executive leadership is constantly shifting, demanding that we adapt not just to its changing tides but to the evolving needs of those we serve. This book is born from a conviction that the highest form of leadership is service, where the greatest success is measured not by individual accolades, but by the collective progress we inspire.

Throughout my career, I have witnessed how visionary leaders harness the power of inclusion, resilience, and authentic communication. Their influence radiates outward, cultivating environments where innovation thrives and every voice finds resonance. These are the leaders who move quietly, shaping futures and uplifting those around them— proof that leadership's true legacy is not found in monuments, but in the lives transformed along the way.

It is my hope that the insights and strategies within these pages become a catalyst for your own growth, whether you are stepping into your first leadership role or refining your craft at the highest echelons. Mastery in leadership calls us to be bold yet compassionate, strategic yet flexible, and always willing to learn from those we lead as much as we guide them. May you find, within these chapters, the tools and inspiration to lead not only with excellence, but with purpose and heart.

Acknowledgements

I am profoundly grateful to my family—my loving husband, Thomas Hollins, and our amazing daughter, Taylor Hollins—for sustaining me, grounding me, and keeping my vision alive. Your unwavering love, patience, and belief in me are daily reminders of why I strive to lead with purpose and integrity.

To my mother, Mattie Jane McGriff Dickey Patterson, whose legacy of education, faith, work ethic, and vision laid the foundation for all that I have accomplished—thank you for showing me that perseverance and courage can turn challenges into opportunities. I also honor my extended family, including my siblings, grandparents, and relatives who nurtured, encouraged, and prayed for me. Each of you played a role in shaping my resilience, my compassion, and my strength.

I am equally indebted to my friends, colleagues, and mentors who stood by me throughout my personal and professional journey. Special thanks to Nancy Cuddihy, Dwight Williams, Anne Kelly (deceased), Dr. Lorna McBarnett (deceased), Major General Roger Brautigan (deceased), and Dr. David Satcher—your mentorship, wisdom, and example have enriched my path and lifted my vision higher. To the countless colleagues and teammates across government, health care, academia, and the military— you have challenged me, supported me, and walked beside me as partners in service and leadership.

To my friends and community, thank you for reminding me of the importance of joy, laughter, and balance. From childhood playmates to lifelong friends, from fellow sailors to professional peers—your encouragement has strengthened me in ways too many to name but never forgotten.

Most importantly, I give glory and honor to God for guiding my steps, removing barriers, surrounding me with grace, and granting me opportunities beyond my imagination. Every success in my journey belongs first to Him, and I remain committed to using the gifts He has entrusted me with to serve others and to uplift future generations.

Book Introduction

In an era defined by relentless technological advances, economic turbulence, and the profound interweaving of global societies, the art and science of leadership is undergoing a radical transformation. This comprehensive guide stands as a beacon for navigating the complexities of modern organizational life, where the power to influence and inspire transcends traditional hierarchies.

The journey begins by tracing the evolution of leadership philosophies, illuminating pivotal movements such as servant leadership, transformational leadership, and adaptive leadership. These foundational frameworks are not mere academic concepts—they are living, breathing models that empower individuals and teams to meet the demands of a dynamic world. The narrative explores how digitalization, automation, and artificial intelligence have fundamentally redefined the very fabric of organizations, compelling leaders to cultivate a harmonious blend of strategic foresight, emotional intelligence, and ethical responsibility.

Throughout the book, readers encounter a rich tapestry of real-world case studies, in-depth interviews, and cutting-edge research from leading institutions like MIT Sloan and Harvard Business School. These stories reveal both triumphs and challenges, offering invaluable lessons on how leaders can foster trust, resilience, and engagement in the face of uncertainty. The text delves into the nuances of remote work and distributed teams, the integration of AI and data-driven decision-making, and the mounting imperative for authentic inclusion, diversity, and belonging at every organizational tier.

What distinguishes this guide is its focus on the lived experiences of innovative CEOs, visionary entrepreneurs, and change agents who have charted bold paths through disruption. Their journeys illustrate the paradoxes of leadership—balancing agility with stability, authority with empathy, and ambition with humility. By distilling these insights, the book equips readers with actionable strategies to lead with purpose, adaptability, and a steadfast commitment to human potential.

Ultimately, this work is more than a manual; it is an invitation to reflect, challenge assumptions, and reimagine what it means to lead in the 21st century. Through its blend of rigorous analysis and inspiring narrative, the book empowers readers to become architects of transformation—guiding their organizations and communities toward a future defined not only by success, but by significance.

"A leader ... is like a shepherd. He stays behind the flock, letting the most nimble go out ahead, whereupon the others follow, not realizing that all along they are being directed from behind."

— Nelson Mandela

Table of Contents

Chapter 1 Building Organizational Capacity: From Individuals to Teams to Networks.. 1

    Introduction 1

    The Foundations of Effective Teams 2

    The Four-Step Process for Capacity Building................. 3

    Capacity Building Training for Networks and Teams 5

    AI in Capacity Building 6

    Developing Leadership Teams for Transformation 8

    Collaboration and Team Dynamics 10

    The Cascading Impact of Leadership............................11

    Case Study: Feedback Mechanisms at Philips............... 12

    The Cost of Inaction vs. the Power of Success............... 13

    Best Practices for the Future.. 13

    Conclusion.. 16

Chapter 2 Employee Engagement and Experience: Key Insights.. 18

    Introduction 18

    Transitioning from Engagement to Experience 19

    Best Practices for Enhancing Employee Experience and Engagement... 21

    The Role of Artificial Intelligence in Employee Experience 22

The Future of Employee Experience...............................22

The Lasting Shift to Employee Experience....................23

Designing Employee Experience for the Future............24

Employee Experience vs. Employee Engagement:
Key Differences 25

Conclusion...27

Chapter 3 Flexible Work Models and Hybrid Work
Culture: Strategic Approaches for Talent Retention............29

Introduction 29

Evolution of Work Models 29

Case Study: Infosys and the Flexibility+ Frame-
work..31

Case Findings and Analysis..31

Discussion 32

Information on AI: 35

Future of Workplace Flexibilities: 36

Conclusion...37

Chapter 4 Inclusive Leadership and Employee
Workplace Well-Being: Best Practices, AI Integration,
and Literature Review..39

Introduction 39

Defining Inclusive Leadership 39

Employee Workplace Well-Being: Dimensions and
Importance 40

Theoretical Foundations 41

Best Practices for Inclusive Leadership.........................41

Workplace Culture: Trends and Priorities for 2026......43

Leveraging Artificial Intelligence in Inclusive
Leadership...46

Challenges to Inclusive Leadership and Employee
Well-Being..47

Case Studies and Applications.....................................48

Metrics for Evaluating Inclusive Leadership.................49

Conclusion..50

Chapter 5 A Journey Through Transformational
Leadership..52

Introduction 52

The Imperative for Transformation.............................53

The Role of Leadership in Transformation 55

From Reactive Managers to Proactive Change
Leaders 56

Vision—The Cornerstone of Transformation 57

Overcoming Resistance & Building Trust.....................58

Communication & Engagement Excellence..................59

Leveraging AI in Transformation Leadership 60

Measuring Success—From Vision to Value 60

Conclusion..63

Chapter 6 Leadership Beyond Job Titles...........................65

Introduction 65

Why Titles No Longer Define Leadership 65

The Foundations Of Leadership Beyond Titles 66

Practices For Leading Without A Title............................68

Case Study — Misuse Of Title Vs. Use Of
   Leadership 69

Modern Research On Leadership & Career
Fulfillment...69

Ai As A Force For Democratized Leadership.................70

Best Practices For Individuals Seeking To Lead
Beyond A Title..71

Conclusion — Leadership As Service, Not Status.........73

Chapter 7 Transforming the Workplace for Generation
Z: A Comprehensive Guide to Engagement, Best
Practices, and AI Integration...75

Introduction 75

Understanding Generation Z in the Workplace 76

Best Practices for Engaging Gen Z.................................76

Integrating Artificial Intelligence: The Future of
Gen Z Engagement...78

Building a Culture of Trust and Authenticity 79

Intergenerational Collaboration: Best Practices 80

Measuring Success: KPIs and Continuous
Improvement..81

Case Studies..81

Practical Toolkit: Templates and Resources..................82

Conclusion: Shaping the Future Together.....................83

Chapter 8 Aligning Talent with the Future of Human Capital Management..85

Introduction: The Shifting Paradigm of Human Capital...85

The Future of Work: Challenges and Opportunities 86

Chart 1: Projected Job Growth and Displacement Due to Automation (2020-2025).................................86

Human + Machine: The Role of AI in Human Capital Management 87

Chart 2: AI Applications in Talent Management...........88

Disruptive Voices: Driving Innovation through Talent..88

Chart 3: Impact of Disruptive Talent on Organizational Performance 89

Best Practices for Hiring and Retention in the Next Decade 89

The Employee Experience: From Onboarding to Advancement... 91

Chart 4: Employee Retention Rates Pre- and Post- Implementation of Career Pathing Programs 91

Engagement and Inclusion: Building Connected, High-Performing Workplaces.......................................92

Data-Driven Decision Making in Human Capital Management...93

Chart 5: Top People Analytics Metrics Used by Leading Organizations 94

Technology Integration: Building the Future
Workplace...95

Case Studies: Organizations Aligning Talent with
Future HCM 96

Conclusion..98

Chapter 9 Leading From The Bottom Up: In-Depth
Section Content...100

Introduction to Leadership Paradigms......................100

The Top-Down Model—Strengths, Weaknesses,
and the Case for Change..101

The Bottom-Up Approach—Principles, Structures,
and Impact 101

Psychological Safety—Building Trust and
Fostering Collaboration 102

AI-Powered Decision-Making—The Digital
Catalyst 103

Advanced Best Practices—Embedding Bottom-Up
Leadership..104

Global and Cultural Perspectives—Tailoring
Leadership Worldwide...104

Remote Work and Technology—Expanding
Possibilities..105

Change Management—From Hierarchy to
Collaboration..106

Leadership Development, Sustainability, and
Future Trends...106

Conclusion..108

Chapter 10 Reflecting on Your Leadership Path: The Modern Leader's Guide 110

    Introduction: The Leadership Journey in a New Era 110

    The Foundations of Modern Leadership 110

    Chart: Leadership Styles (2025) 111

    AI and the Future of Leadership...................................112

    Chart: AI Applications in Leadership 112

    Self-Reflection in Leadership.......................................113

    Communication Challenges and Solutions...................114

    Chart: Communication Tools for Leaders 115

    Building and Sustaining Culture...................................115

    Collaboration in the Age of AI......................................116

    Chart: Collaboration Metrics (Sample Data)...............116

    Skill Building for Tomorrow's Leaders 117

    Chart: Top Skills for 2025 Leaders 117

    Best Practices in Leadership Today 118

    Case Study: AI-Driven Leadership Transformation.....118

    The Role of Mentorship and Peer Networks 119

    Conclusion: Charting Your Path Forward 120

Chapter 11 The Imperative for Resilient, Servant Leadership...121

    Introduction 121

    Why Resilience Matters 122

    Pillars of Resilient Leadership 123

Servant Leadership as a Resilience Multiplier 124

Embedding Resilience Across Teams 125

Leading Through AI-Enhanced Disruption 126

Measuring Organizational Resilience 127

Case Studies of Resilient Leadership 127

Key Takeaways for Leaders 128

Conclusion 129

Book Summary A Guide to Leadership in a
Transforming World 131

Book References.. 133

The Author 143

About the Author 147

Chapter 1

Building Organizational Capacity: From Individuals to Teams to Networks

Comprehensive Strategies for Organizational Growth and Leadership Transformation

Introduction

In today's rapidly evolving business environment, the success of an organization often depends on its ability to adapt, collaborate, and foster innovation at every level. Building organizational capacity is not a single initiative, but rather a continuous process that requires a strategic, team-based approach. Actual capacity building is rooted in the deliberate cultivation of collective buy-in and the establishment of a clear, shared vision for the future.

Organizations that thrive in times of uncertainty do so because they empower teams to gather information, devise solutions, implement actions, and continually refine outcomes. This chapter examines a comprehensive approach to developing organizational capacity, highlighting the crucial role of leadership teams and the cascading impact of their behaviors and decisions throughout the organization.

The Foundations of Effective Teams

Understanding Team Dynamics

Addressing how a team behaves is not about getting leaders to like one another or always agree. Rather, it is about fostering a culture where everyone feels encouraged to put issues on the table, tackle problems collectively, make prompt decisions, and remain committed to each person's success. Effective teams recognize that healthy tension and debate fuel innovation, leading to better outcomes.

Creating Rules and Mechanisms for Accountability

A critical component for effective teams is the establishment of explicit norms and mechanisms that make it comfortable for members to seek help or hold one another accountable. For example, at Philips, executive committee off-sites use "speed-dating"-style feedback exercises. Each day, every member connects with five others and exchanges two things: an appreciative comment and a suggestion for growth. This practice not only builds trust but also ensures that feedback is frequent, actionable, and part of the team's routine.

Psychological Safety and Open Communication

Teams perform best when psychological safety is prioritized. Members must feel confident that they can speak candidly, share concerns, and propose new ideas without fear of retribution. Leaders play a crucial role in modeling transparency, encouraging authenticity, and acknowledging contributions. When communication is open and honest, teams are better equipped to resolve issues quickly and innovate together.

The Four-Step Process for Capacity Building

1. Launch Teams Quickly and Build as You Go

Organizational agility depends on the rapid formation of teams. Establishing a central hub to coordinate activities, with smaller, cross-functional teams operating as spokes, allows for both alignment and autonomy. Team leaders should be selected for their creativity, critical thinking, resilience, and problem-solving skills. These small, skill-diverse groups can move quickly from planning to action. Once formed, teams should be empowered to make decisions within their scope, avoiding unnecessary bureaucracy or delays.

As teams launch, it is essential to foster an environment that encourages experimentation and allows lessons to be learned from setbacks. Progress is prioritized over perfection, and teams are expected to iterate and adapt as they move forward.

2. Enable Autonomy While Staying Connected

As teams take shape, maintaining strong connections both within and across teams is crucial. Regular communication with the central hub—such as through daily stand-up meetings or weekly retrospectives—ensures that information flows freely and alignment is maintained. Leaders serve as both catalysts and coaches: they facilitate opportunity identification, spark creativity, provide necessary resources, and offer guidance when obstacles arise.

Rather than micromanaging, effective leaders enable teams to operate independently within clear boundaries, stepping in only when needed to resolve issues or remove obstacles. This balance of autonomy and connection drives both accountability and innovation.

3. Champion Transparency and Authenticity

Transparency is the foundation of trust and rapid decision-making. Organizations benefit when information is shared openly, and when individuals are recognized for taking calculated risks. Authentic communication—where leaders and team members speak honestly about challenges, failures, and successes—creates a psychologically safe culture that encourages continuous improvement.

Leaders should model vulnerability by admitting mistakes and sharing what they have learned. Recognizing the efforts of those who innovate or take well-considered risks, even if outcomes are uncertain, reinforces a growth mindset and empowers others to do the same.

4. Promote Self-Organization

Once networks of teams are established, the next challenge is to promote self-organization. While the central hub continues to provide strategic direction and support, teams are encouraged to manage themselves, develop their own solutions, and maintain connections with other groups. Self-organizing teams are resilient, adaptive, and capable of sustaining high performance over time.

Leaders facilitate this transition by modeling the desired behaviors, recognizing innovation and risk-taking, and ensuring that insights and lessons are shared transparently across the organization.

Capacity Building Training for Networks and Teams

Developing Skills and Mindsets

Capacity building is most effective when it is intentional and inclusive. Training must focus not only on technical competencies but also on developing the mindsets and behaviors that enable success in teams within networks. Key focus areas include leadership, resilience, management, innovation, infrastructure, governance, and support systems.

Engagement, teamwork, and inclusion are also critical. Teams must be empowered to leverage the full spectrum of skills, experiences, and perspectives available within the organization. Tailored training programs and ongoing developmental support ensure that all members are equipped to make meaningful contributions to collective goals.

Building Infrastructure and Support Systems

Effective networks and teams require robust support systems. This includes tools and processes for communication, knowledge sharing, and project management, as well as access to resources and expertise. Leadership must invest in the infrastructure that enables collaboration and innovation at scale.

Governance structures should be straightforward but flexible, providing enough oversight to ensure alignment without stifling creativity or agility.

AI in Capacity Building

Integrating Artificial Intelligence to Enhance Organizational Capabilities

Artificial Intelligence (AI) is reshaping the landscape of capacity building across organizations. By harnessing the power of machine learning, advanced analytics, and intelligent automation, organizations can accelerate learning, generate insights, and optimize team performance in ways previously unimaginable.

Application of AI in Team Development

- Talent Management: AI-driven tools can identify skill gaps, recommend personalized learning paths, and help match individuals to teams where their unique strengths are most needed. This ensures that talent is deployed efficiently and that individuals continue to grow within the organization.

- Collaboration Platforms: AI-enabled collaboration platforms facilitate better communication, automate routine work, and flag emerging issues for teams to address quickly. These platforms analyze team interactions, provide feedback on dynamics, and suggest strategies to improve effectiveness.

- Feedback and Coaching: AI systems can aggregate feedback from multiple sources, analyze patterns, and help leaders deliver targeted coaching. By providing objective, data-driven assessments, AI enhances the feedback process and ensures that development is ongoing and equitable.

- Continuous Learning: AI-powered content curation and adaptive learning platforms deliver training tailored to individual learning styles and needs, making capacity building scalable and efficient.

- Predictive Analytics: AI tools can forecast team performance, identify risks, and simulate outcomes of strategic decisions, enabling proactive interventions and more confident leadership.

Challenges and Considerations

While AI presents immense opportunities, organizations must also address concerns around privacy, ethical use of data, and the risk of over-reliance on algorithms. Human judgment, empathy, and creativity remain irreplaceable, and AI should be viewed as a complement to—not a substitute for—human leadership and collaboration.

Capacity building strategies must incorporate clear guidelines for the responsible use of AI, ensuring transparency, fairness, and inclusivity throughout the organization.

Future Directions

As AI technologies continue to evolve, their role in capacity building will expand. Organizations that can integrate AI thoughtfully into their leadership, team development, and training processes will position themselves to thrive in a dynamic and complex world.

Developing Leadership Teams for Transformation

Reinventing Purpose and Driving Change

Transformation in a modern organization begins with a leadership team willing to rethink its purpose and the very nature of how it creates value. This means looking beyond digitization to consider how leadership roles must evolve, how teams are constructed, and how the organization responds to complexity and ambiguity.

Leaders must start by identifying which roles are truly critical for the company's strategic future. These may include nontraditional positions aligned with emerging needs and opportunities.

Assembling Diverse and Capable Teams

Assembling a leadership team is about more than filling seats. It requires intentionally bringing together individuals with the right mix of skills, backgrounds, and experiences. The goal is to build a team capable of balancing seemingly paradoxical leadership behaviors—such as being decisive yet open to debate, or driving performance while fostering inclusion—and challenging each other to achieve extraordinary results.

Diversity in thought, experience, and expertise is essential, and truly inclusive teams are better equipped to anticipate challenges, identify opportunities, and drive innovation.

Focusing the Leadership Team on Transformation

Leadership teams must focus on transformation rather than merely operational responses. This requires dedicating time and energy to defining a bold agenda, launching ambitious initiatives, and monitoring progress. Change must be driven from the top, but it also needs to be supported throughout the organization. The behaviors, priorities, and commitments of the C-suite will set the tone for the entire enterprise.

It is critical that these leaders not only articulate a vision but also empower others to act. Leaders must hold themselves and their teams accountable for both outcomes and how those outcomes are achieved.

Ownership and Collaboration

Owning the team's behavior means taking responsibility for both successes and setbacks. It also means fostering a culture of honest feedback, mutual support, and continuous improvement. Collaboration is at the heart of effective leadership teams: members work together to solve problems, challenge assumptions, and drive progress.

Tools like regular feedback exercises—such as those used by Philips, where leaders share appreciative comments and suggestions for growth—can help build trust and accountability.

Collaboration and Team Dynamics

Balancing Daily Operations with Future Building

Leadership teams must strike a balance between managing day-to-day operations and building for the future. This dual focus requires aligning all members around a shared understanding of necessary changes and the organization's unique potential.

Pairing executives for cross-functional collaboration enables the merging of different strengths, a more profound mutual understanding, and more creative solutions to complex problems. Such pairings also help break down silos and encourage holistic thinking.

Prioritizing Open Communication and Mutual Success

The most effective teams are those where open communication is prioritized, issues are addressed quickly, and members are committed to each other's success. When trust is high and feedback is routine, teams move faster, make better decisions, and deliver stronger results.

By defining bold agendas and launching transformative initiatives, leadership teams set the pace and direction for the entire organization.

The Cascading Impact of Leadership

The Role of the C-Suite in Organizational Transformation

A major transformation cannot be achieved solely by the top team. The new kind of leadership must cascade downward, building leadership muscle throughout the entire organization. The process begins in the C-suite, where leaders must surround themselves with talented individuals who can balance paradoxical behaviors and challenge each other to collectively accomplish significant goals.

The leadership team must set aside dedicated time and energy to define strategy, drive initiatives, and exemplify the behaviors they wish to see throughout the company. Failure to do so risks stagnation and lost opportunity, while success positions the firm to excel in an increasingly complex world.

Embedding Leadership Behaviors Across the Organization

The behaviors and priorities set at the top establish expectations for all teams and employees. Through intentional modeling, coaching, and reinforcement of desired behaviors—such as open dialogue, accountability, and inclusion—leaders make it possible for new ways of working to take root.

Training and development programs should be designed to equip leaders at every level with the skills and mindsets needed for transformation. By empowering teams, providing ongoing feedback, and celebrating progress, organizations ensure that their leadership framework is robust and resilient.

Case Study: Feedback Mechanisms at Philips

Implementing Speed-Dating-Style Feedback

One practical example of effective feedback mechanisms comes from Philips, where the executive committee integrates speed-dating-style feedback sessions during off-site meetings. Each day, every member is required to connect with five other members, offering one appreciative comment and one suggestion for professional growth.

This structured yet informal approach normalizes feedback, strengthens relationships, and ensures that development is an ongoing, collective process. The result is a leadership team that is more cohesive, supportive, and open to growth.

Lessons Learned from Structured Feedback

The Philips model highlights the importance of creating routines that make feedback natural and expected. By embedding these practices into the leadership team's rhythm, organizations can foster more open communication, accelerate growth, and improve overall performance.

The Cost of Inaction vs. the Power of Success

The Risks of Failing to Lead Effectively

Failing to invest in leadership and capacity building can be a costly mistake. Teams that lack clear direction and accountability struggle to make informed decisions, effectively address problems, and achieve desired results. In contrast, organizations with strong leadership teams are equipped to handle complexity, drive innovation, and sustain high performance over time.

Positioning for Long-Term Success

Organizations that prioritize leadership development and team effectiveness position themselves to thrive in an increasingly complex and competitive landscape. By aligning around bold goals, empowering teams, and cascading effective behaviors, these organizations ensure that they are prepared for both the challenges and opportunities of the future.

Best Practices for the Future

Embrace Continuous Learning and Adaptation

Organizations must foster a culture of continuous learning, encouraging teams to regularly update their skills and knowledge in response to shifting market dynamics and technological advances. This can be achieved through ongoing education, peer-to-peer learning, and the use of AI-powered, personalized training modules.

Strengthen Engagement, Teamwork and Inclusion

Enhancing engagement, teamwork, and inclusion is vital for long-term organizational growth. Teams should actively involve all members, foster a sense of belonging, and ensure that everyone's contributions are valued. Collaborative environments encourage open dialogue, shared accountability, and collective problem-solving. By emphasizing inclusion, organizations unlock the full potential of their people, fostering trust and encouraging diverse perspectives. Best practices include implementing team-building activities, creating opportunities for cross-functional collaboration, and ensuring equitable access to resources and opportunities for advancement.

Adopt Agile Operating Models

Agile methodologies empower organizations to respond swiftly to change. Encourage flexibility in team structures, decision-making processes, and project management practices to foster a more adaptable and effective approach. Regular retrospectives and feedback loops ensure that organizations remain agile and continually improve.

Leverage Technology Responsibly

Use digital tools and AI to enhance collaboration, productivity, and decision-making, but always pair technological solutions with human judgment and ethical oversight. Prioritize transparency, privacy, and responsible data use to build trust within and outside the organization.

Promote Psychological Safety and Well-being

Prioritize the psychological safety and well-being of all team members. Encourage open communication, celebrate vulnerability, and provide support systems to address stress and burnout. A healthy and resilient workforce is a foundation for sustainable success.

Model Integrity and Accountability

Leaders must consistently model integrity and accountability, setting clear expectations and adhering to their commitments. By holding themselves and others to high standards, leaders foster a culture of trust and reliability.

Invest in Leadership Development

Commit to developing current and future leaders through mentorship, coaching, and experiential learning. Tailored programs help leaders grow the capabilities needed to guide teams through complexity and change.

Conclusion

Building organizational capacity is an ongoing journey that starts with leadership but extends to every team and individual within the company. By fostering open communication, prioritizing psychological safety, enabling autonomy, embedding feedback mechanisms, and integrating artificial intelligence, organizations create the foundation for sustained growth and innovation. The commitment to developing leadership at all levels and following best practices is what ultimately distinguishes organizations that succeed in today's complex world and remain prepared for the future.

"People don't care how much you know until they know how much you care."

— John Maxwell

Chapter 2

Employee Engagement and Experience: Key Insights

Introduction

This chapter highlights how organizations can boost employee engagement and experience by fostering effective communication, empathetic leadership, and positive work cultures. Leaders who prioritize emotional intelligence, respect, and inclusivity help build trust and resilience, while modern businesses are shifting from annual surveys to holistic approaches that use data, collaboration, and employee feedback to shape strategies tailored for different staff groups.

Best practices include regular feedback, recognition, flexible work options, career growth support, well-being initiatives, psychological safety, and digital tools. Artificial intelligence further enhances personalization and proactive solutions. The evolving workplace now emphasizes technology-led personalization, hybrid work models, holistic well-being, and purpose-driven cultures. Understanding the difference between employee engagement (commitment and satisfaction) and employee experience (the full journey and shared responsibility) is crucial. Ultimately, ongoing dialogue and strategic investment in meaningful experiences drive higher engagement and long-term success.

Leveraging Communication During Challenging Times

Victoria Zambito, SVP at Vector Solutions, emphasizes the importance of clear and consistent communication in organizations, especially during times of uncertainty or crisis. Quick adaptation, transparent processes, and regular touchpoints with leadership are vital. Teams should regularly review communications and marketing efforts for sensitivity and responsiveness, utilizing data analytics and available resources to support stakeholders. Optimism and a resilient, inclusive culture are encouraged as guiding principles.

Essential Leadership Skills for Challenging Times

Christopher Rios from Blue Rock Search highlights core leadership qualities for a positive customer experience: communication, emotional intelligence, kindness, and respect. These attributes foster trust, provide necessary feedback, and support team growth, emphasizing that soft skills are often more valuable than technical expertise for building a healthy organizational culture.

Transitioning from Engagement to Experience

Moving Beyond Employee Engagement

While many companies still rely on annual engagement surveys, data shows that only about half of employees feel engaged at work. Modern approaches advocate for a focus on employee experience (EX), which more holistically drives motivation and retention. Examples like United Overseas

Bank demonstrate how deeper HR strategies across the employee lifecycle can lead to improved engagement scores.

Lessons for Building a Positive Employee Experience

- Partner with an EX Coach or Expert: Leverage professional planning guidance, executing, and assessing EX strategies.

- Collaborate Across Functions: Bring together business units, technology, and communication teams, supported by EX champions gathering feedback and evolving strategies.

- Design for Employees: Direct input from employees in policy creation ensures relevance, as seen with feedback-driven remote work policies.

- Tailor Approaches: Address the unique needs of each employee segment, from new hires to senior leaders, recognizing that one size does not fit all.

- Maintain Dialogue: Two-way communication fosters a culture of continuous improvement and responsiveness.

Collectively, these lessons build the foundation for impactful EX strategies that drive productivity and engagement.

Best Practices for Enhancing Employee Experience and Engagement

- Listen and Act: Regularly gather employee feedback and visibly act on it to build trust and demonstrate organizational commitment.

- Recognize and Reward: Celebrate achievements, both big and small, to boost morale and engagement.

- Embrace Flexibility: Promote work-life balance through flexible schedules and remote options tailored to employee needs.

- Support Development: Offer training, mentorship, and career progression opportunities for continuous employee growth.

- Invest in Well-being: Implement holistic health and wellness programs addressing physical, mental, and emotional health.

- Ensure Psychological Safety: Foster an environment where employees can voice ideas, take risks, and innovate without fear.

- Leverage Digital Tools: Provide easy-to-use platforms for collaboration, productivity, and communication.

The Role of Artificial Intelligence in Employee Experience

Artificial Intelligence (AI) is revolutionizing how organizations understand and improve employee experience. By harnessing AI-powered analytics and predictive modeling, companies can identify trends in engagement, retention, and productivity with greater accuracy. AI-driven features—such as Intelligent Nudges, action planning, and dynamic feedback collection—enable managers to tailor interventions and measure their impact in real time. These capabilities not only streamline decision-making but also allow organizations to proactively address issues, personalize employee journeys, and cultivate a thriving workforce. The integration of AI into platforms like People Insights empowers organizations to fine-tune their culture and practices for optimal results continually.

The Future of Employee Experience

The future of employee experience is poised for transformation as organizations adapt to rapid technological, social, and economic changes. Several key trends are shaping what lies ahead:

- Personalization Through Technology: The next wave of employee experience will see greater personalization, with platforms leveraging AI, machine learning, and advanced analytics to deliver tailored feedback, development opportunities, and engagement strategies based on individual preferences and career aspirations.

- Hybrid and Flexible Work Models: The normalization of remote and hybrid work will demand new approaches to inclusion, collaboration, and well-being as employees seek greater autonomy and balance in their work lives.

- Holistic Well-being: Organizations will expand their focus beyond physical health to include mental, emotional, and financial well-being. Providing resources, support, and a culture that prioritizes holistic health will become a core differentiator.

- Continuous Listening and Real-Time Feedback: Advances in employee listening tools will make it possible to gather and act on feedback in real time, creating more responsive and adaptive organizations.
- Purpose-Driven Culture: Employees are increasingly seeking meaningful work that aligns with their values. Organizations must articulate and embody a clear purpose to attract and retain top talent.

As the workforce evolves, those organizations that proactively invest in employee experience—through technology, leadership, and culture—will be best positioned to adapt, succeed, and foster lasting engagement.

The Lasting Shift to Employee Experience

Historical Perspective and Today's Trends

Workplace improvements in the twentieth century focused on safety and comfort, but primarily addressed practical needs. The evolution toward engagement aimed to benefit both workers and organizations, although it was limited as a standalone metric. The rise of employee experience, pioneered by organizations such as Airbnb, places people and their holistic journey at the center of workplace strategy.

Defining Employee Experience

According to Susan Peters (GE), employee experience is "seeing the world through the eyes of our employees." Jacob Morgan argues that practices should be redesigned to suit people rather than the organization. Research confirms that positive employee experience correlates with higher engagement and retention.

Designing Employee Experience for the Future

Personalization and Purpose

Employees seek trust, recognition, meaningful collaboration, growth opportunities, and a clear sense of purpose. Organizations must shift away from top-down policies and design authentic, personalized experiences.

Systematic Approach to EX

Design thinking, supported by data and empathy, ensures employees are central to problem-solving. Success depends on a clear vision, understanding employee needs, and enabling digital journeys.

Three Steps for Effective EX Transformation

- Establish a Baseline: Align leaders, assess employee needs, and set clear organizational goals for EX.

- Transform Employee Journeys: Design impactful experiences by focusing on "moments that matter" and leveraging digital tools.

- Equip the Organization: Provide scalable systems and tools for transforming and measuring employee experience.

Success Factors

EX strategies require clear goals, personalized journeys, robust analytics, and cross-functional coalitions. Rigorous measurement and continuous improvement are key to adaptation and success.

Employee Experience vs. Employee Engagement: Key Differences

Definitions and Relationship

Employee engagement is the emotional commitment to one's work and organization, driven by motivation, pride, and a desire for retention. Employee experience is the comprehensive journey, encompassing relationships, environment, resources, and opportunities.

Comparing Scope, Timeframe, Responsibility, and Measurement

Aspect	Employee experience	Employee engagement
Scope	Entire employee journey from onboarding to exit	Level of commitment to job roles
Timeframe	Long-term, linking past and future experiences	Current state of engagement
Responsibility	Shared among leaders and HR	Primarily manager-driven
Measurement	Ongoing feedback and lifecycle touchpoints	Surveys on satisfaction and commitment

Methods for Measuring and Improving Employee Experience and Engagement

- Anonymous employee engagement surveys

- Lifecycle assessments to track experience at every stage

- HR metrics analysis (retention, turnover, etc.)

- Frequent and consistent measurement intervals

- Open dialogue via feedback sessions and regular meetings

Systematic analysis enables targeted improvements and sustained progress.

Conclusion

Building a positive employee experience is essential for achieving high employee engagement. Through thoughtful strategies, attentive listening, and the innovative use of technology, organizations can inspire and retain a motivated, productive workforce, ultimately achieving lasting business success.

"Leaders honor their core values, but they are flexible in how they execute them."

- Colin Powell

Chapter 3

Flexible Work Models and Hybrid Work Culture: Strategic Approaches for Talent Retention

Introduction

The workplace has undergone radical changes over the past decade, spurred by technological advances and the global COVID-19 pandemic. Remote and flexible working, once considered a privilege, has become a standard expectation for many employees. The rise of remote work, hybrid office models, and gig-based employment marks a shift away from traditional 9-to-5 routines, redefining how organizations attract, engage, and retain talent in a dynamic labor market.

Evolution of Work Models

From Traditional to Hybrid Structures

Work models have evolved from physical, centralized office arrangements to remote and now hybrid options. The adoption of information and communication technologies, accelerated by the pandemic, proved remote work feasible at scale, leading to the widespread adoption of hybrid models that balance flexibility with collaboration. These shifts challenge old ideas about productivity and presence, demanding new strategies for team management, communication, and culture.

Psychological Contracts in Flexible Work

The implicit agreements between employers and employees—psychological contracts—have changed. Employees now seek autonomy, trust, and work-life integration, rather than just job security and pay. Flexible arrangements support this shift, and organizations that violate these new expectations by reverting to rigid policies risk disengagement and higher attrition.

Generational Preferences

Different generations have distinct expectations: Millennials and Gen Z value flexibility, mental health, and purposeful work, while older generations often prefer more structured, in-person environments. To remain competitive, organizations must design inclusive work environments that address these diverse needs.

Impact of Hybrid Work

Research shows that productivity often equals or surpasses in-office performance when employees have autonomy over their schedules. Engagement increases with trust and support, though hybrid work can also introduce challenges such as isolation and digital fatigue. Organizations that invest in digital infrastructure, psychological safety, and leadership development report higher employee satisfaction and performance.

Case Study: Infosys and the Flexibility+ Framework

Infosys Limited, a global IT leader, transitioned from a traditional office-based model to a hybrid system in response to the pandemic. Internal surveys revealed that 65% of employees preferred hybrid work, and 72% identified flexibility as a top retention factor. In 2022, Infosys launched the "Flexibility+ Framework," allowing employees to split their time between office and remote work, investing heavily in digital infrastructure and introducing satellite work hubs to reduce commute times.

The company shifted to outcome-based performance evaluations and promoted internal mobility through a talent marketplace. Well-being initiatives, such as counseling and mental health days, were prioritized. These efforts led to a 22% decrease in attrition among employees aged 25–35, an 18% rise in employee satisfaction, and a 12% productivity increase in agile teams.

Case Findings and Analysis

Flexibility as a Retention Factor

Flexible work was a primary reason employees chose to stay at Infosys. Autonomy over work location and schedule led to increased organizational commitment, especially among younger professionals.

Job Satisfaction, Loyalty, and Productivity

Hybrid work improved job satisfaction, loyalty, and productivity, driven by better work-life balance, reduced commuting, and more opportunities for career growth.

Implementation Barriers

Challenges included the need for large investments in technology, the complexity of standardizing hybrid policies, and resistance from some leaders accustomed to in-person management. Cultural shifts and aligning hybrid work with client expectations also required careful management.

Generational and Gender Considerations

Millennials and Gen Z responded most positively to flexible arrangements. The adoption of hybrid work enabled a significant increase in women returning from career breaks, but also highlighted the need for inclusive policies to ensure equal visibility and advancement opportunities.

Discussion

The Infosys example supports research showing that flexible work models, when implemented thoughtfully, enhance productivity, retention, and inclusion. Success depends on trust, autonomy, digital investment, and ongoing manager training. Flexible work also contributes to diversity, equity, and inclusion by reducing barriers for underrepresented groups, though care must be taken to address potential inequities in visibility and advancement.

Strategic Recommendations

- Customize hybrid policies by role and department.

- Invest in robust digital infrastructure and employee well-being.

- Train leaders to manage hybrid and distributed teams with trust-based evaluation.

- Establish feedback mechanisms to continually refine hybrid models.

- Account for sectoral and geographic limitations in policy design.

- Address potential biases in feedback and survey data.

- Be prepared to adapt as hybrid work evolves over time.

Impact of Hybrid Work Strategies on Organizational Outcomes

Hybrid Strategy	Short-Term Effect	Long-Term Benefit	Measurement Metric
Role-Specific Customization	Improved employee engagement	Higher retention rates	Turnover statistics
Digital Infrastructure Investments	Increase in productivity	Scalability and resilience	System uptime; output per employee
Employee Well-Being Initiatives	Reduced absenteeism	Enhanced job satisfaction	Well-being survey results
Leadership Training	Stronger team cohesion	Effective distributed management	Manager performance reviews
Continuous Feedback Mechanisms	Quicker issue resolution	Ongoing improvement in work models	Feedback cycle times
Bias Mitigation	More equitable participation	Greater diversity and inclusion	DEI metrics
Adaptability	Effective response to change	Organizational resilience	Change management success rate

Ongoing improvement in work models	Feedback cycle times		
Bias Mitigation	More equitable participation	Greater diversity and inclusion	DEI metrics
Adaptability	Effective response to change	Organizational resilience	Change management success rate

Best Practices:

- Foster transparent communication channels and regular check-ins to support continuous feedback and improvement.

- Implement structured mentorship and sponsorship programs to elevate underrepresented voices and drive measurable progress on DEI metrics.

- Engage employees in the design and assessment of flexible work policies, ensuring their lived experiences inform organizational decisions.

- Use data-driven approaches to monitor, evaluate, and refine change management processes for greater resilience.

Information on AI:

Artificial intelligence is increasingly shaping workplace processes. AI-powered analytics can pinpoint bottlenecks in feedback cycles, uncover patterns in participation and inclusion, and automate routine tasks. AI-driven platforms enable unbiased resume screening and support adaptive scheduling, helping organizations mitigate bias and optimize talent utilization. Machine learning models can also forecast workforce needs and inform strategic decisions about remote work, hybrid models, and well-being initiatives.

Future of Workplace Flexibilities:

The future of flexible work will be characterized by personalization, inclusivity, and agility. Organizations are investing in technologies that enable seamless collaboration across geographies, time zones, and work styles. Flexible scheduling, remote and hybrid options, and results-focused performance measures are expected to become standard. Embracing asynchronous work and leveraging digital platforms will enhance productivity while supporting employee autonomy and well-being. Forward-thinking companies will prioritize trust, outcome-based management, and continuous learning to thrive in a rapidly evolving environment.

Conclusion

Flexible and hybrid work models are now strategic imperatives for attracting and retaining talent. These models strengthen the psychological contract between employers and employees, supporting autonomy, well-being, and professional growth. While challenges remain—such as technological gaps and ensuring equity—organizations that prioritize flexibility, ongoing feedback, and inclusivity will be poised for long-term resilience and success in the evolving world of work.

"If your actions inspire others to dream more, learn more, do more and become more, you are a leader."

– Unknown.

Chapter 4

Inclusive Leadership and Employee Workplace Well-Being: Best Practices, AI Integration, and Literature Review

A Comprehensive Analysis

Introduction

Inclusive leadership has emerged as a critical factor in promoting employee workplace well-being, especially as organizations become more diverse and technologically advanced. This chapter provides an in-depth analysis of inclusive leadership, its impact on employee well-being, best practices, the role of artificial intelligence (AI), and references from current academic literature.

Defining Inclusive Leadership

Inclusive leadership refers to the behaviors and strategies that leaders employ to create an environment where all employees feel valued, respected, and empowered to contribute. It transcends traditional leadership models by actively fostering diversity and psychological safety.

Key Characteristics of Inclusive Leaders

- Empathy: Understanding and addressing employee needs and concerns.

- Openness: Encouraging diverse perspectives and ideas.

- Fairness: Ensuring equitable opportunities and resources for all.

- Collaboration: Facilitating teamwork across different backgrounds.

- Accountability: Holding oneself and others responsible for inclusive behaviors.

Employee Workplace Well-Being: Dimensions and Importance

Well-being at work encompasses physical, psychological, and social factors that contribute to an employee's overall health and productivity. It's a multidimensional construct comprising:

- Physical Well-Being: Health, safety, and ergonomics.

- Psychological Well-Being: Stress reduction, mental health support, and emotional resilience.

- Social Well-Being: Belonging, positive relationships, and meaningful collaboration.

Research, such as Liu et al. (2024), demonstrates a strong correlation between inclusive leadership and improved employee vigor, engagement, and well-being.

Theoretical Foundations

Inclusive leadership draws from several theoretical frameworks:

- Social Identity Theory: Recognizes the impact of group membership on self-concept and behavior.

- Leader-Member Exchange Theory: Focuses on the quality of relationships between leaders and individual employees.

- Positive Organizational Scholarship: Highlights strengths-based approaches to workplace management.

Best Practices for Inclusive Leadership

1. Foster Psychological Safety

Encourage employees to speak up without fear of retribution. Leaders should:

- Model vulnerability by admitting mistakes and seeking feedback

- Actively listen and validate diverse viewpoints.

- Implement regular check-ins and open forums for discussion.

2. Cultivate Cultural Competence

Develop leaders' ability to understand, communicate with, and effectively interact with people across cultures. This includes:

- Providing training on unconscious bias and intercultural communication.

- Celebrating cultural events and holidays in the workplace.

- Developing multicultural teams and promoting cross-functional collaboration.

3. Encourage Supervisor Developmental Feedback

According to Liu et al. (2024), developmental feedback from supervisors enhances employee vigor and well-being. Best practices include:

- Delivering regular, constructive feedback focused on growth.

- Setting clear expectations and personal development goals.

- Recognizing achievements and identifying opportunities for improvement.

4. Promote Equity and Accessibility

Ensure that resources, opportunities, and rewards are distributed fairly. Leaders should:

- Establish transparent policies for promotions and compensation.

- Provide reasonable accommodations for employees with disabilities.

- Monitor data for gaps in access or representation.

5. Invest in Well-Being Programs

Integrate physical and mental health programs into organizational culture:

- Offer wellness initiatives, such as exercise classes, mindfulness sessions, and nutrition workshops.

- Provide access to mental health resources and counseling.

- Encourage work-life balance through flexible scheduling and remote work options.

Workplace Culture: Trends and Priorities for 2026

- Workplace culture stands as the heartbeat of every successful organization, shaping employee engagement, innovation, and retention. More than a mere buzzword, it reflects the values and priorities that guide teams in their daily collaboration and long-term vision. Robust, values-driven cultures consistently yield higher productivity and satisfaction among employees. A global survey in 2024 revealed that 83% of respondents consider a positive workplace culture a key factor in their decision to remain with their employer.

- Recent research underscores the pivotal role of inclusive leadership in fostering environments where employees experience well-being, vigor, and psychological safety. According to Liu et al. (2024), inclusive leadership—coupled with developmental feedback—can nurture employee resilience and engagement. Shore et al. (2018) and Randel et al. (2018) highlight how workplaces that celebrate belonging and the value of uniqueness encourage collaboration and adaptability.

- The priorities shaping organizational culture in 2025 are reflected in the following table:

Element	Percentage of Organizations Prioritizing
Well-being	72%
Culture & Purpose	68%
Leadership	65%
Inclusion	61%
Employee Experience	70%
Communication & Voice	56%
Society & Sustainability	48%

- These priorities manifest through initiatives such as mental health programs, diversity-focused leadership development, and sustainability pledges. The following table shows the growing emphasis on employee well-being and experience over recent years:

Year	% of Companies with Wellbeing Programs	% of Companies Enhancing Employee Experience
2022	54%	60%
2023	61%	65%
2024	69%	67%
2025	72%	70%

- The rise of AI in leadership (Zhu & Li, 2021) and the emphasis on psychological safety in teams (Edmondson, 1999), as well as the adaptation of inclusive practices for virtual workforces (Raghuram et al., 2019), further illustrate the dynamic strategies organizations employ to strengthen their cultures.

- Ultimately, cultivating workplace culture is an ongoing journey. Leveraging best practices, investing in employee well-being, and fostering inclusive leadership positions organizations for sustained success. As emphasized in the conclusion, continuous learning, adaptation, and accountability are essential for nurturing and maintaining inclusive environments in an ever-evolving world.

Leveraging Artificial Intelligence in Inclusive Leadership

AI technologies present new opportunities and challenges for inclusive leadership.

AI-Driven Talent Management

AI can analyze workforce data to identify trends, predict turnover, and recommend interventions. Advanced algorithms may help:

- Reduce bias in recruitment by anonymizing applications and standardizing evaluations.

- Map employee skills and suggest targeted learning opportunities.

- Monitor employee well-being through sentiment analysis and engagement surveys.

AI for Personalized Feedback and Development

Machine learning systems can provide tailored feedback based on employee performance data. Benefits include:

- Automated coaching and mentoring systems that adapt to individual needs.

- Real-time analytics on team dynamics and well-being indicators.

- Digital platforms for goal-setting and progress tracking.

Ethical Considerations

While AI brings efficiency, it raises important ethical issues:

- Protecting employee privacy and data security.

- Ensuring transparency in AI decision-making processes.

- Mitigating algorithmic bias that may perpetuate inequalities.

Challenges to Inclusive Leadership and Employee Well-Being

Despite its benefits, inclusive leadership faces several obstacles:

- Resistance to Change: Some employees or managers may be hesitant to adopt new inclusive practices.

- Implicit Bias: Unconscious prejudices can undermine well-intentioned policies.

- Resource Limitations: Small or underfunded organizations may struggle to implement comprehensive programs.

- Globalization: Leading across borders requires heightened sensitivity to cultural differences.

Case Studies and Applications

Company A: Global Tech Firm

Implemented AI-powered feedback tools to support developmental reviews and track employee well-being. Resulted in:

- 30% improvement in employee engagement scores.

- Reduced attrition rates among underrepresented groups.

Company B: Healthcare Organization

Launched inclusive leadership training and invested in mental health support. Outcomes included:

- Significant reduction in workplace stress and absenteeism.

- Greater innovation through diverse teams.

Metrics for Evaluating Inclusive Leadership

Organizations should track progress using quantitative and qualitative indicators:

- Employee Engagement Surveys

- Turnover and Retention Rates

- Diversity Representation in Leadership

- Participation in Well-Being Programs

- Feedback Quality and Frequency

Conclusion

Inclusive leadership forms a cornerstone for employee workplace well-being, driving engagement, innovation, and resilience. Integrating best practices, leveraging emerging AI tools, and grounding actions in ethical considerations empower organizations to cultivate workplaces where every employee thrives. Continuous learning, adaptation, and accountability are essential for sustaining inclusive environments in a rapidly evolving world.

"What you do has far greater impact than what you say."

– Stephen Covey

Chapter 5

A Journey Through Transformational Leadership

Disrupt to Thrive: Mastering Transformation Leadership in 2025

Introduction

The accelerating pace of change driven by technological innovation, market volatility, and evolving workforce expectations has made transformation leadership a core competency rather than a specialized skill. Once episodic, transformation is now continuous; leaders must consistently guide their organizations through disruption with vision, empathy, and agility. Research by McKinsey (2018) shows that transformations with actively engaged sponsors are **2.5 times more likely to succeed**, and Prosci (2022) confirms that **leadership engagement is the single greatest factor influencing employee adoption**.

This chapter consolidates contemporary research, industry case studies, leadership theory, and modern practices into a unified, practical guide for executives, change sponsors, and transformation practitioners navigating organizational change in 2025 and beyond. It integrates the origins of transformational leadership (Burns, 1978; Bass, 1985), contemporary applications, AI-enabled leadership tools, and real-world examples from global companies including Apple, Amazon, Coca-Cola, and Netflix.

The Imperative for Transformation

Transformation today is not merely a strategic option—it is a survival requirement. Organizations across industries face continuous pressure from:

Key Drivers of Transformation

- **Digital Disruption**: Rapid emergence of AI, automation, cloud, and machine learning (McKinsey, 2018).

- **Customer-Centric Expectations:** Heightened demand for personalization, immediacy, and purpose-driven brands.

- **Globalization:** Increasingly complex supply chains, geopolitical risks, and regulatory complexity.

- **Workforce Shifts:** Rise of remote work, cross-generational teams, and demand for meaningful engagement.

Common Barriers to Transformation

Barrier	Impact	Recommended Response
Lack of Executive Sponsorship	Stalled initiatives	Engage sponsors early; clarify roles
Unclear Vision	Misalignment, resistance	Co-create and communicate vision
Employee Resistance	Low morale, delays	Listen actively; address concerns; highlight early wins
Poor Communication	Misinformation	Multi-channel communication strategy
Insufficient Resources	Burnout, budget overruns	Invest in skills, tech, support structures

Harvard Business Review emphasizes that resistance is often rooted not in opposition but in fear, uncertainty, and lack of clarity (HBR, 2018).

The Role of Leadership in Transformation

Transformational leadership extends beyond oversight—leaders set direction, model desired behaviors, and create a culture where innovation thrives.

Core Responsibilities of Transformation Leaders

1. **Vision Creation:** Crafting an inspiring, coherent vision aligned with environmental realities.

2. **Strategic Alignment**: Ensuring functions understand their role in delivering the vision.

3. **Active Sponsorship**: Demonstrating commitment through action, visibility, and resourcing.

4. **Trust Building**: Creating psychological safety (Edmondson, 2018) for experimentation and honest communication.

5. **Continuous Measurement**: Tracking real-time adoption, engagement, progress, and obstacles.

Case Example:
A Fortune 500 company reduced resistance by **45% in 12 months** by deploying change ambassadors, facilitating listening sessions, and reinforcing positive behaviors.

From Reactive Managers to Proactive Change Leaders

Organizations evolve most effectively under leaders who anticipate disruption rather than respond to it.

Leadership Maturity Progression

Stage	Characteristics	Outcomes
Reactive	Responds when issues occur	Inconsistent results
Responsive	Plans for anticipated change	Improved resilience
Proactive	Drives change and shapes future direction	Sustained success

Proactive Leadership Practices

- Scenario planning using predictive analytics
- Cross-functional stakeholder engagement
- Innovation labs for prototyping
- Empowerment-based decision-making
- Insights-driven leadership dashboards

Vision—The Cornerstone of Transformation

A clear, compelling vision is strongly correlated with transformation success; McKinsey (2018) reports organizations with strong visions outperform peers by **3×**.

Effective Vision Framework

Step	Description
Vision Statement	Clear, aspirational future direction
Strategic Priorities	Focus areas required to achieve the vision
Operational Initiatives	Programs aligned to strategic priorities
KPIs & Outcomes	Quantifiable indicators of success

Vision Co-Creation

- Partner with leaders, employees, and customers
- Leverage data and trend analysis
- Use storytelling to provide an emotional connection

Diagram: Vision Cascade Model

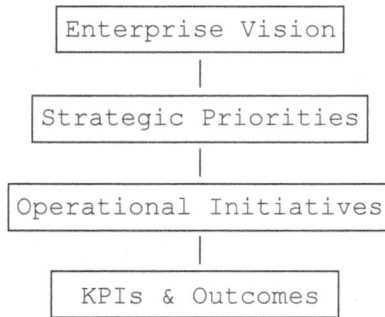

```
┌─────────────────────┐
│  Enterprise Vision  │
└─────────────────────┘
           │
┌─────────────────────┐
│ Strategic Priorities │
└─────────────────────┘
           │
┌─────────────────────┐
│ Operational Initiatives │
└─────────────────────┘
           │
┌─────────────────────┐
│   KPIs & Outcomes   │
└─────────────────────┘
```

Overcoming Resistance & Building Trust

Resistance is normal and predictable (Prosci, 2022). Leaders who approach resistance with empathy strengthen resilience.

Strategies for Reducing Resistance

- **Active listening** through forums, focus groups, pulse surveys
- **Influencer mapping** to identify informal champions
- **Early wins** to showcase tangible benefits
- **Transparent risk conversations**
- **Peer networks and coaching programs**

Trust is built not through perfection but through consistency, transparency, and intentional relationship-building.

Communication & Engagement Excellence

Communication is the engine that moves transformation from strategy to action.

Key Communication Methods

- **Audience segmentation** (executives, managers, frontline teams, customers)
- **Storytelling** to contextualize change
- **Synchronous & asynchronous channels**
- **Feedback loops** that respond visibly to input

Channel Comparison Chart

Channel	Strength
Face-to-face	High trust, real-time clarity
Workshops	Creativity, collaboration
Digital platforms	Broad reach, consistency
Email/newsletters	Documentation, regular cadence

Leveraging AI in Transformation Leadership

AI is redefining how leaders plan, communicate, and measure change.

AI Applications Supporting Transformation Leadership

- **Predictive analytics** for adoption forecasting
- **Sentiment analysis** to detect morale shifts
- **Change impact modeling**
- **Automated communication assistants**
- **Personalized learning paths** for employees

AI Adoption Stages

Stage	Description
Exploration	Identify AI opportunities
Pilot	Small-scale testing
Scalability	Expand successful use cases
Full Integration	Enterprise-wide embedding

Measuring Success—From Vision to Value

Measurement transforms the transformation from aspiration into evidence.

Measurement Categories

- **Balanced scorecards** (financial, operational, customer, and behavioral)
- **Pulse surveys** on readiness, sentiment, trust
- **Benchmarking** against industry leaders
- **Continuous improvement cycles**

Common KPIs

KPI	Definition
Employee Engagement Score	Support for and participation in transformation
Time-to-Value	Speed of impact realization
Cost Savings	Financial benefits
Customer Satisfaction	Impact on experience
Innovation Pipeline	Volume & quality of ideas

Future of Transformational Leadership (2025–2030)

Emerging trends shaping the next decade:

1. AI-Augmented Leadership

Leaders will co-lead transformations with AI systems that forecast disruption and personalize interventions.

2. Human-Centered Transformation

Empathy, inclusion, and psychological safety will become non-negotiable leadership traits.

3. Skills-Based Leadership

Organizations will shift toward skills marketplaces and internal talent ecosystems.

4. Ecosystem Transformation

Cross-industry collaboration will replace isolated corporate strategies.

5. Radical Transparency

Real-time dashboards will make vision, progress, and decisions visible to all employees.

Best Practices for Transformation Leaders

1. **Lead with Vision and Clarity**
2. **Co-Create Strategy with Stakeholders**
3. **Model the Desired Behaviors**
4. **Communicate Early and Often**
5. **Empower Teams Through Autonomy and Trust**
6. **Use Data to Drive Decisions**
7. **Celebrate Early Wins**
8. **Maintain Psychological Safety**
9. **Enable Continuous Learning**
10. **Integrate Human + Digital Transformation**

Conclusion

The most effective transformation leaders are those who blend **strategic vision**, **empathy**, **communication excellence**, and **data-driven decision-making**. Rooted in the foundational principles of Burns, Bass, and modern leadership science—and strengthened by new AI-powered capabilities—transformational leadership enables organizations to thrive in uncertainty. Leaders who embrace this approach create cultures where people feel valued, innovation is continuous, and transformation becomes not a disruption but a competitive advantage.

"Leadership is not about a title or a designation. It's about impact, influence, and inspiration."

– Robin S. Sharma

Chapter 6
Leadership Beyond Job Titles

Introduction

Leadership has traditionally been equated with authority, hierarchy, and position. Yet modern organizations have evolved beyond rigid structures—placing greater value on personal influence, emotional intelligence, and shared purpose. This chapter examines leadership as a human capability rather than a job designation. Drawing from contemporary research, workplace observations, and expert perspectives, we explore the deeper ethos of leading beyond titles and why the future of leadership depends on character, connection, and service over status.

Why Titles No Longer Define Leadership

In an era of flattened organizations, hybrid teams, automation, and distributed decision-making, titles have lost their historic power. As Sanborn (2024) notes, titles confirm leadership but do not create it. Instead, relevance is driven by capability, trust, and contribution. Employees increasingly follow those who demonstrate integrity, purpose, and clarity rather than those who simply occupy higher positions.

A more adaptive definition of leadership centers on influence, not authority. A leader is someone who moves people—emotionally, cognitively, or behaviorally—toward shared goals (Maxwell, 2020).

This view positions leadership as a discipline practiced daily, not something bestowed by a corner office.

Story: The Credit Union "Hidden Leaders"

A powerful illustration comes from a financial institution where the most influential individuals were not the executives but tenured staff with no formal authority. These individuals became "the go-to people"—trusted for guidance, problem-solving, and clarity. Their leadership emerged from expertise, emotional intelligence, and genuine commitment to coworkers.

They demonstrated a universal truth:

Leadership is an inside-out process.

It begins with mindset, expands through behaviors, and is confirmed by impact—not by job description.

The Foundations Of Leadership Beyond Titles

1. Influence Over Authority

Leadership rooted in influence emphasizes purpose, alignment, and interpersonal trust. Unlike command-based leadership, this form relies on authenticity and consistent values-driven behavior (Wojnicki, 2024). Influence is earned through action, not enforced through position.

2. Character and Integrity

Integrity forms the backbone of real leadership. In volatile environments, people look not for perfection but for stability, accountability, and transparency. Leaders who anchor decisions in principle reinforce trust and enhance team resilience.

3. Emotional Intelligence

Emotional intelligence (EQ) is a central predictor of leadership effectiveness (Goleman, 2018). Leaders with high EQ listen deeply, interpret cues, manage conflict constructively, and foster psychological safety—turning workplaces into collaborative communities rather than transactional environments.

4. Vision Beyond Goals

True leadership communicates purpose that transcends tasks. Hoffman (2023) stresses that vision binds teams together, inspiring alignment and innovation. Effective leaders anchor work to meaning, helping individuals see how their contributions matter.

5. Courage, Especially in Crisis

Titles often dissolve in crisis, revealing leaders who step forward with clarity, empathy, and decisiveness. Courageous leaders embrace candid dialogue, navigate uncertainty, and empower others to do the same.

Chart: Shifting Sources Of Leadership Credibility

(Conceptual Chart)

- 1980s–1990s: Authority → Hierarchy → Seniority

- 2000s: Expertise → Process Control → Performance

- 2010s: Collaboration → Innovation → EQ

- 2020s–Future: Influence → Trust → Vision → Alignment

This progression highlights that contemporary leadership is defined less by structure and more by humanity.

Practices For Leading Without A Title

Andrea Wojnicki (2024) identifies five practices that enhance leadership credibility irrespective of role:

1. Demonstrate People Leadership

Support, mentor, and elevate others. Create followership by modeling professionalism and care.

2. Be Proactive

Leadership is future-oriented. Anticipate opportunities, innovate workflows, and identify emerging needs before they are assigned to you.

3. Create Thought Leadership

Share insights in meetings, publish ideas, and become known for a domain of expertise.

4. Communicate with Confidence

Confidence—both internal mindset and external presence—builds credibility and inspires trust.

5. Talk Leadership

Language shapes perception. Articulating your leadership journey influences how others perceive your role.

Case Study — Misuse Of Title Vs. Use Of Leadership

Hoffman's experience as a systems administrator demonstrates the consequences of title-based leadership. A newly hired supervisor abruptly shifted the project direction without consultation, explanation, or shared ownership. This eroded morale, dismantled trust, and ultimately led team members to leave the organization.

The lesson: Title-based decisions without influence or communication undermine leadership effectiveness.

Modern Research On Leadership & Career Fulfillment

A 2023 study in the International Journal of Environmental Research and Public Health found that long-term career satisfaction correlates more strongly with alignment between strengths, values, and roles—not with title or pay grade. When individuals can influence their environment and contribute meaningfully, engagement rises significantly.

This reinforces that leadership is a lived capability—not a hierarchical reward.

Chart: Drivers Of Career Fulfillment

- Meaningful contribution
- Value alignment
- Autonomy
- Influence and impact
- Supportive relationships
- Psychological safety
- Title and compensation (moderate correlation)

Ai As A Force For Democratized Leadership

AI is reshaping leadership dynamics by:

1. Expanding Access to Insight

AI tools provide real-time analytics, coaching simulations, and decision-support once available only to executives.

2. Enabling Small Teams to Lead Big

AI acts like a "co-founder," allowing individuals with no formal authority to execute complex strategies, coordinate teams, and amplify their impact.

3. Enhancing Emotional Intelligence

AI-driven sentiment analysis and conversational coaching help leaders improve communication, self-awareness, and conflict management.

4. Flattening Hierarchies

As AI handles administrative authority-based tasks, human leadership shifts toward influence, intuition, and creativity—traits accessible to anyone.

Vision of the Future:

Leadership becomes a shared capability practiced across levels, not a privilege granted to a few.

Best Practices For Individuals Seeking To Lead Beyond A Title

- Lead where you are—act with ownership before you are formally given it.

- Prioritize relationships; influence grows through trust.

- Align actions with values to maintain integrity.

- Mentor others; coaching fosters credibility and community.

- Build thought leadership to amplify impact.

- Communicate clearly, consistently, and confidently.

- Use your strengths intentionally and visibly.

- Seek opportunities that expand—not just elevate—your career.

Conclusion — Leadership As Service, Not Status

Leadership is not defined by the words printed under your name on a business card but by the feeling you leave in the room when you exit. The greatest leaders inspire belief, unlock potential, and elevate others. Their power is measured not in authority but in impact.

As Robin Sharma famously said:

"Leadership is not about a title or a designation. It's about impact, influence, and inspiration."

The future of leadership belongs to those who serve with clarity, courage, and character—regardless of their title.

"If your actions inspire others to dream more, learn more, do more and become more, you are a leader."

– Unknown

Chapter 7

Transforming the Workplace for Generation Z: A Comprehensive Guide to Engagement, Best Practices, and AI Integration

Redefining Organizational Culture for the Future Workforce

Introduction

The modern workplace is at a crossroads, shaped by demographic shifts, rapid technological advances, and the growing influence of Generation Z. As this new cohort enters the workforce with fresh expectations, values, and talents, organizations must rethink their strategies to create environments where Gen Z not only works but thrives. This guide synthesizes research, expert perspectives, actionable best practices, and transformative technological solutions to help organizations harness the full potential of Gen Z, build intergenerational relationships, and future-proof their talent strategies.

Understanding Generation Z in the Workplace

- Background: Born between the mid-1990s and early 2010s, Gen Z is the most diverse, digitally native, and socially conscious generation yet.

- Values: Authenticity, inclusion, mental well-being, agency, and social impact.

- Work Preferences: Flexibility, transparency, meaningful work, and technological integration.

Organizations must recognize Gen Z's desire for agency and meaningful contribution. This is a generation eager to co-create the future, expecting workplaces to reflect their identity, values, and ambitions.

Best Practices for Engaging Gen Z

1. Co-Creation and Agency

- Implement participatory decision-making: Invite Gen Z employees to ideation sessions, strategy workshops, and innovation labs.

- Establish feedback loops: Use digital platforms and AI-powered surveys to gather real-time input from Gen Z staff, ensuring their voices shape organizational priorities.

- Best Practice Case Study: Companies like Google and Salesforce have launched "employee innovation councils" where Gen Zers help steer product development.

2. Reverse-Mentoring Programs

- Promote bidirectional learning: Pair Gen Z employees with senior staff to foster mutual learning and understanding.

- Leverage AI-based skill mapping: Match mentors and mentees based on complementary expertise and interests.

Best Practice: Deloitte Digital's reverse-mentoring initiatives have improved digital literacy among senior leaders while empowering Gen Zers.

3. Influencer Engagement

- Identify internal and external Gen Z influencers: Use AI tools to analyze social media, project outcomes, and peer nominations.

- Empower influencers as culture shapers: Involve them in change management, onboarding, and DEI task forces.

4. Foster Inclusion and Well-Being

- Design mental health support programs tailored for Gen Z, leveraging digital health platforms.

- Develop transparent policies on diversity, equity, and inclusion, with AI-assisted bias detection in recruitment and promotion.

5. Flexibility and Digital Fluency

- Transition to hybrid and remote work models, supported by AI-based productivity and collaboration tools.

- Invest in continuous training on emerging technologies, including AI, machine learning, and automation.

Integrating Artificial Intelligence: The Future of Gen Z Engagement

AI is rapidly reshaping the workplace, offering opportunities to personalize experiences, enhance productivity, and support Gen Z's tech-forward orientation.

AI Use Cases

- Recruitment: AI algorithms can screen applicants for skills and cultural fit, helping organizations identify top Gen Z talent.

- Onboarding: Personalized AI chatbots guide new hires through processes, policies, and resources.

- Performance Management: Real-time feedback platforms powered by AI allow Gen Z employees to track progress and set goals.

- Career Pathing: AI recommends learning modules, mentorships, and project opportunities based on individual strengths and aspirations.

Ethical Considerations and Human-Centered AI

- Ensure transparency and fairness in algorithmic decisions.

- Involve Gen Z in the design and deployment of AI systems.

- Continuously monitor for bias and unintended consequences.

Reference: Dunlop, A. (2021). Elevating the Human Experience: Three Paths to Love and Worth at Work.

Building a Culture of Trust and Authenticity

Trust is the cornerstone of Gen Z engagement. Leaders must cultivate environments where Gen Z feels seen, heard, and empowered.

Strategies

- Communicate openly and honestly about organizational challenges and opportunities.

- Create safe spaces for dialogue, feedback, and experimentation.

- Recognize and celebrate individuality and diversity.

Reference: Dunlop, A. & Hatfield, S. (2022). The Four Factors of Trust: How Organizations Can Earn Lifelong Loyalty.

Intergenerational Collaboration: Best Practices

The future workplace will be intergenerational. Organizations must bridge gaps between Gen Z and other cohorts through intentional practices.

Key Actions

- Facilitate cross-generational teams using collaborative tech platforms.

- Develop training modules to enhance empathy and understanding between groups.

- Host regular "future of work" roundtables featuring voices from all generations.

Measuring Success: KPIs and Continuous Improvement

- Employee Engagement Scores: Track Gen Z satisfaction using AI-powered analytics.

- Retention Rates: Monitor turnover and conduct exit interviews focused on Gen Z perspectives.

- Innovation Output: Quantify Gen Z contributions to product, service, and process improvements.

Case Studies

Author	Title	Year	Focus
Amelia Dunlop	Elevating the Human Experience	2021	Love and worth at work
Michael Pankowski	Engaging Gen Z	2021	Gen Z engagement strategies
Deloitte Digital	Future of Work Reports	2022	Workforce trends and technology
Steven Hatfield	The Four Factors of Trust	2022	Organizational trust-building

Practical Toolkit: Templates and Resources

- Reverse-Mentoring Program Template

- AI-Driven Feedback Survey Example

- Internal Gen Z Influencer Identification Checklist

- Sample Hybrid Work Policy for Gen Z

Conclusion: Shaping the Future Together

Each challenge and gap is an invitation—an opportunity to forge meaningful connections and co-create a workplace where Gen Z and every generation can flourish. By embracing best practices, leveraging AI, and building trust, organizations can achieve enduring success and innovation.

"Effective leadership is not about making speeches or being liked; leadership is defined by results not attributes."

– Peter Drucker

Chapter 8

Aligning Talent with the Future of Human Capital Management

Strategic, Technological, and Human-Centric Approaches for the Next Decade

Introduction: The Shifting Paradigm of Human Capital

The field of human capital management (HCM) is in a state of continual transformation, propelled by advances in technology, changes in workforce demographics, and evolving employee expectations around flexibility, purpose, and growth. Digital transformation and artificial intelligence (AI) are rapidly altering traditional processes, driving organizations to re-examine talent strategies from the ground up. In this comprehensive chapter, we explore practical, evidence-based approaches for aligning talent with the needs of tomorrow, drawing from thought leadership, recent conferences, and cutting-edge research.

The Future of Work: Challenges and Opportunities

1.1 The Changing Nature of Jobs

Over the next five years, automation and AI are forecasted to reshape the global labor market. The World Economic Forum anticipates that by 2025, 85 million roles may be displaced by technology, while 97 million new jobs will emerge—mostly in knowledge-intensive and technology-driven fields. This transition demands a radical rethink of job design, with a premium placed on digital fluency, creativity, complex problem-solving, and emotional intelligence.

1.2 The Imperative for Agility

To remain competitive, organizations must encourage agility at every level. This includes cultivating a workforce adept at rapid learning, adapting to new tools, and moving seamlessly between projects. Key strategies include developing flexible talent pipelines, creating continuous reskilling and upskilling programs, and fostering cultures where experimentation and iteration are rewarded.

Chart 1: Projected Job Growth and Displacement Due to Automation (2020-2025)

Year	Jobs Displaced	Jobs Created
2020	12	15
2023	55	62
2025	85	97

Human + Machine: The Role of AI in Human Capital Management

2.1 AI in Recruitment and Selection

AI technologies are revolutionizing recruitment, enabling faster sourcing, unbiased screening, and predictive assessments. Tools like machine learning algorithms analyze candidate data for potential, fit, and future performance. Video interviewing platforms now use natural language processing to flag potential red flags and identify promising behavioral traits.

2.2 AI for Employee Engagement

Digital assistants, real-time pulse surveys, and conversational analytics track employee sentiment and engagement. Advanced analytics help HR leaders intervene early when morale dips, personalize communication, and foster inclusive environments by surfacing and addressing systemic issues.

2.3 AI in Learning and Development

Adaptive learning management systems customize training recommendations to individual needs, optimizing skill growth and retention. AI-driven platforms offer microlearning, gamification, and career pathing features that help employees visualize and actualize their potential within the organization.

Chart 2: AI Applications in Talent Management

Application	Key Benefit	Adoption Rate (%)
Recruitment	Streamlined Screening	65
Engagement	Real-time Feedback	48
Learning & Development	Personalized Training	52

Disruptive Voices: Driving Innovation through Talent

3.1 Embracing Non-Traditional Talent

Mike Walsh, keynote speaker at the SHRM Talent 2025 conference, advocates for hiring disruptors—individuals who question norms and drive change. These "reward hackers" maximize efficiency and offer fresh perspectives, enabling organizations to adapt quickly in a competitive landscape.

Best Practices for Fostering Innovation Teams:

- Actively recruit individuals from diverse backgrounds and industries to infuse new thinking.

- Establish forums and channels for open debate and constructive dissent, celebrating creative risk-taking.

- Reward employees for experimentation, fast learning, and challenging existing processes.

- Regularly rotate team members across projects to foster cross-pollination of ideas and prevent silos.

Chart 3: Impact of Disruptive Talent on Organizational Performance

Metric	Traditional Teams	Innovation Teams
Time to Market (months)	18	10
Revenue Growth (%)	5	13
Employee Engagement (%)	67	79

Best Practices for Hiring and Retention in the Next Decade

4.1 Strategic Sourcing and Employer Branding

Digital tools and analytics enable organizations to precisely target ideal candidates and build dynamic talent pipelines. Strong employer branding—conveyed through authentic stories, employee testimonials, and online platforms—attracts candidates whose values align with organizational culture.

- Leverage social media and digital campaigns to showcase diversity, innovation, and growth opportunities.

- Deploy AI-powered sourcing tools to identify passive candidates and expand reach.

- Gather and analyze candidate feedback to fine-tune messaging and recruitment strategies.

- Invest in virtual recruiting events and immersive digital onboarding experiences.

4.2 Personalized Employee Experience

Retaining top talent means investing in tailored, flexible work options, individualized development plans, and recognition programs.

- Offer remote and hybrid work arrangements, flexible hours, and adaptive benefits packages.

- Establish mentorship, coaching, and sponsorship initiatives that foster personal and professional development.

- Celebrate achievements and milestones publicly, using digital platforms and in-person events.

- Encourage open feedback and give employees an active voice in shaping policies and processes.

The Employee Experience: From Onboarding to Advancement

5.1 Onboarding for Success

A strategic onboarding process blends digital orientation modules with interactive experiences. Assigning peer mentors, leveraging mobile apps for task management, and gamifying learning help new hires adjust quickly and become productive members of the team.

5.2 Continuous Development and Career Pathing

Organizations that prioritize upskilling and transparent career pathing outperform peers in retention and engagement. Personalized learning platforms, regular career conversations, and clear advancement criteria empower employees to take charge of their growth.

Chart 4: Employee Retention Rates Pre- and Post-Implementation of Career Pathing Programs

Year	Pre-Implementation	Post-Implementation
2022	70	-
2023	-	81
2024	-	84

Engagement and Inclusion: Building Connected, High-Performing Workplaces

6.1 Employee Engagement Initiatives

Sustained engagement is essential for productivity and satisfaction. High-performing organizations regularly assess engagement through digital surveys, pulse checks, and analytics. Actionable feedback leads to improvements in work-life balance, workload distribution, and recognition practices.

- Set clear engagement goals and track progress using dashboards and analytics.

- Implement recognition platforms that highlight contributions across teams and geographies.

- Conduct quarterly engagement surveys and act on results to demonstrate commitment to employee voice.

- Facilitate transparent communication between leaders and teams.

6.2 Inclusion and Belonging

Inclusion is about ensuring every employee feels valued, respected, and empowered to contribute. Inclusive workplaces foster creativity, resilience, and higher retention.

- Provide training on inclusive leadership, cultural competence, and unconscious bias mitigation.

- Establish employee resource groups and peer networks to support underrepresented communities.

- Promote transparent promotion and leadership selection processes to minimize bias.

- Encourage cross-functional collaboration and diverse project teams.

Leaders must cultivate psychological safety, ensuring all voices—especially those from different backgrounds—are genuinely heard and considered in decision-making.

Data-Driven Decision Making in Human Capital Management

7.1 Leveraging Analytics for Insight and Action

People analytics is increasingly central to HR strategy. By tracking turnover, engagement, diversity, and performance, companies can make data-driven decisions about hiring, promotion, and retention.

- Utilize predictive analytics to forecast attrition and proactively address risk factors.

- Visualize trends through dashboards, enabling targeted interventions.

- Share insights regularly with stakeholders, driving transparency and continuous improvement.

- Benchmark progress against industry standards and competitors.

Chart 5: Top People Analytics Metrics Used by Leading Organizations

Metric	Usage (%)
Turnover Rate	91
Engagement Score	88
Diversity Ratio	73
Performance Index	82

Technology Integration: Building the Future Workplace

8.1 Cloud, Mobile, and Social Platforms

Modern HCM systems are cloud-based for scalability and security, with mobile-first interfaces for remote and hybrid work. Social feedback platforms encourage transparency and foster a sense of community.

- Adopt robust Human Resources Information System (HRIS) systems with integrated modules for payroll, performance, and learning.

- Encourage mobile access to HR tools so employees can manage benefits, time off, and training from anywhere.

- Use collaborative platforms to support project management and team communication.

- Integrate social recognition systems to boost engagement.

8.2 Cybersecurity and Data Privacy

HR leaders must prioritize data privacy, ensuring compliance with regulations like General Data Protection Regulation (GDPR) and various regulated privacy acts. This includes regular audits, clear data governance policies, and ongoing training for staff on security best practices.

- Partner with IT for secure data storage, access, and backup.

- Regularly update software and conduct security drills to guard against breaches.

- Educate employees about privacy policies and their rights regarding personal information.

Case Studies: Organizations Aligning Talent with Future HCM

9.1 Case Study: Google—People Analytics as a Strategic Driver

Google's approach to people analytics includes rigorous experimentation, A/B testing on HR policies, and transparent sharing of findings. This data-centric culture has driven improvements in hiring accuracy, leadership development, and retention rates.

9.2 Case Study: Unilever—Building a Culture of Continuous Learning

Unilever's digital learning initiatives provide employees with tailored content, social learning opportunities, and career navigation tools. Their focus on lifelong learning has increased internal mobility and reduced skill gaps.

9.3 Case Study: Salesforce—Engagement as a Business Imperative

Salesforce invests in engagement through frequent feedback, recognition programs, and career growth opportunities. Their "Ohana" culture underscores inclusion and belonging, resulting in consistently high employee satisfaction and innovation metrics.

Conclusion

Human capital management is characterized by ongoing transformation, propelled by rapid advancements in digital technologies and artificial intelligence. This dynamic environment continues to redefine the future of work, introducing both challenges and opportunities as job roles evolve. To navigate these changes successfully, organizations must promote agility at every level, leveraging insights from data analysis in areas such as job growth, talent management, retention rates, and data-driven decision-making. The chapter presented a thorough discussion on the influence of disruptive talent and the identification of best practices for future workforce strategies. Furthermore, it underscored the significance of engagement and inclusion in a perpetually changing world, highlighting their collective benefits for all humankind. Several case studies were also examined, spanning multisector workforces and encompassing multigenerational individuals, teams, and groups, thereby illuminating the complex and multifaceted nature of contemporary human capital management.

"You may not control all the events that happen to you, but you can decide not to be reduced by them."

– Maya Angelou

Chapter 9

Leading From The Bottom Up: In-Depth Section Content

Expanding on the Structure and Practice of Bottom-Up Leadership

Introduction to Leadership Paradigms

Traditionally, leadership has been pictured as a solitary figure at the helm of an organization—making critical decisions, charting the course, and shouldering the weight of responsibility. This archetype persists in the classic "top-down" structure, where direction, strategy, and vision descend from executives to every layer below. Yet, as economies, markets, and technologies evolve, so too must our approach to organizational leadership. The "bottom-up" model is gaining ground, representing a shift toward unlocking the collective intelligence and creativity that reside throughout the workforce. This section explores the historical roots, cultural influences, and contemporary pressures that drive the need for more inclusive, participatory leadership models in modern organizations.

The Top-Down Model—Strengths, Weaknesses, and the Case for Change

In a top-down system, authority is concentrated at the highest tiers. This can bring about decisive action during crises, ensure consistency across large organizations, and clarify lines of accountability. However, when leaders operate at a distance from day-to-day realities, blind spots emerge. Employees on the front lines may feel their insights are undervalued, resulting in disengagement or resistance to top-level directives. Innovation may be stifled if only a select few are entrusted with decision-making, and the organization becomes less agile in the face of rapid change.

Aspect	Top-Down Leadership	Bottom-Up Leadership
Decision-Making	Centralized, hierarchical	Decentralized, collaborative
Employee Role	Task execution	Idea generation, shared ownership
Adaptability	Slower, less responsive	Faster, more innovative
Morale	Potential for disengagement	Higher engagement

The Bottom-Up Approach—Principles, Structures, and Impact

Bottom-up leadership transforms the organizational landscape by recognizing and harnessing the expertise of those who interact with problems and opportunities daily. Here, leadership is less about issuing commands and more about facilitating collective action, enabling employees to propose solutions and implement change. In such organizations, communication flows both ways—managers listen, adapt, and support. Structures are often flatter, teams are given clear autonomy, and everyone is encouraged to contribute ideas, fostering a sense of ownership and accountability.

This model not only nurtures innovation but can also help organizations respond more rapidly to market shifts, customer needs, and internal challenges. As every employee becomes a potential change agent, the entire organization becomes more resilient and adaptable.

Psychological Safety—Building Trust and Fostering Collaboration

For bottom-up leadership to thrive, psychological safety must be a foundational value. Without it, team members may hesitate to share new ideas or respectfully challenge the status quo. Psychological safety is cultivated when leaders demonstrate openness, humility, and genuine interest in learning from others. Practical steps include inviting questions, rewarding curiosity, and normalizing mistakes as opportunities for learning. Amy Edmondson's research shows that high psychological safety correlates with higher engagement, better risk management, and more effective problem-solving.

Factor	Low Safety	High Safety
Idea Generation	Limited	Robust
Employee Turnover	High	Low
Innovation Rate	Stagnant	Accelerated

AI-Powered Decision-Making—The Digital Catalyst

Artificial intelligence (AI) is reshaping organizations by augmenting human insight with data-driven analysis. In a bottom-up environment, AI tools democratize access to business intelligence, allowing employees to surface trends, identify pain points, and propose strategic improvements regardless of their position within the hierarchy. For example, predictive analytics can help sales teams anticipate client needs, while collaborative platforms enable engineers to co-create solutions in real time across continents. The challenge lies in promoting transparency in algorithms, managing ethical risks, and ensuring all teams have the training and access needed to benefit from these technologies.

AI Tool	Benefit	Potential Risk
Predictive Analytics	Empowers employee insights	Data bias, overreliance
Collaborative Platforms	Cross-functional teamwork	Privacy concerns
Automated Reporting	Reduces admin burden	Loss of nuance

Advanced Best Practices—Embedding Bottom-Up Leadership

To institutionalize bottom-up leadership, organizations must create systems that support continuous development and transparent measurement. Peer mentoring, cross-functional training, and leadership development programs foster skill growth and psychological safety. Recognition programs—especially those leveraging AI for unbiased, real-time feedback—encourage experimentation and initiative. Clear, accessible dashboards help employees monitor their progress toward shared goals, while open forums for idea submission ensure that good ideas never go unheard.

Year	Training Hours	Skill Proficiency (%)
2022	16	58
2023	27	76

Global and Cultural Perspectives—Tailoring Leadership Worldwide

Culture shapes every facet of leadership, from how decisions are made to how dissent is voiced. In Scandinavian countries, consensus and egalitarianism are deeply rooted, resulting in high levels of trust and engagement. In Japan, the Kaizen philosophy and continuous feedback cycles drive meticulous improvement. African organizations often leverage the power of mobile connectivity and crowdsourcing to adapt quickly to changing markets. Multinational organizations must customize their bottom-up practices to local values and regulatory environments, creating a mosaic of leadership strategies that reflect the diversity of their workforce.

Region	Main Approach	Key Benefit
Scandinavia	Consensus, flat hierarchy	High engagement
Japan	Feedback loops, Kaizen	Continuous improvement
Africa	Mobile crowdsourcing	Market agility

Remote Work and Technology—Expanding Possibilities

The shift to remote and hybrid work, accelerated by global events like the COVID-19 pandemic, has fundamentally changed the way organizations operate. Digital platforms and cloud-based tools now connect teams from across the globe, enabling asynchronous collaboration and constant access to information. However, physical distance can create challenges in building rapport and shared culture. Leaders must be intentional about establishing regular communication routines, providing digital training, and facilitating virtual spaces for informal interaction. By leveraging technology, organizations can maintain high engagement and collaborative energy, regardless of location.

Change Management—From Hierarchy to Collaboration

Transitioning to a bottom-up model is a significant organizational change that demands vision, persistence, and careful management. Using change frameworks—such as Kotter's 8-Step Process—can help leaders navigate resistance, align incentives, and sustain momentum. This involves building a coalition of champions, painting a compelling vision, securing early wins, and embedding new behaviors into the organization's DNA. Leaders must address legacy mindsets, provide continuous training, and ensure open channels for feedback and adaptation.

Barrier	Mitigation Strategy
Hierarchical culture	Training, open communication
Lack of trust	Relationship building, feedback systems
Technology gaps	Invest in AI tools, education

Leadership Development, Sustainability, and Future Trends

Leadership development is no longer confined to the C-suite. Forward-thinking organizations nurture leadership potential at all levels through rotational programs, reverse mentoring, and personalized learning pathways. AI-driven talent analytics help identify emerging leaders and align development opportunities with organizational needs. Bottom-up leadership also enhances sustainability and corporate social responsibility, empowering teams to propose and drive green initiatives. Looking ahead, organizations will increasingly blend top-down oversight with the innovation and agility of bottom-up participation, using AI to support seamless connectivity and collective intelligence.

Year	Emerging Leaders Identified	Leadership Program Graduates
2022	34	21
2023	51	32
Year	Engagement Score (Top-Down)	Engagement Score (Bottom-Up)
2021	62	N/A
2022	65	70
2023	N/A	78
Organization Type	AI Adoption Rate (%)	Reported Innovation Growth (%)
Top-Down	38	12
Bottom-Up	61	27

When organizations embrace bottom-up leadership, they unlock reservoirs of creativity, adaptability, and engagement. Supported by a culture of trust, cutting-edge technologies, and best practices tailored to diverse contexts, these organizations are well-positioned for sustained success in an ever-changing world.

Conclusion

This chapter provides an in-depth examination of the transformation in leadership paradigms, specifically the shift from traditional top-down models to bottom-up approaches. The analysis addresses the merits and drawbacks of both methods, presenting a compelling case for change while detailing the principles, organizational structures, and impact inherent in bottom-up leadership. Emphasis is placed on the imperative to support the well-being and safety of the workforce as organizations transition, underscoring the responsibility of leaders to foster a secure and supportive environment during periods of change.

Furthermore, the chapter highlights the integration of AI-powered decision-making and shares best practices from global and cultural perspectives. It extends the discussion to encompass the evolving landscape of remote work and workplace flexibility, considering their implications for performance and generational well-being. The significance of adaptability, change management, leadership development, and sustainability is reiterated, positioning these elements as essential to growth, competitiveness, and long-term organizational success.

"If you are not willing to learn, no one can help you. If you are determined to learn, no one can stop you."

– Zig Ziglar

Chapter 10

Reflecting on Your Leadership Path: The Modern Leader's Guide

Insights, Strategies, and the Role of AI in Shaping Leadership Skills for 2025

Introduction: The Leadership Journey in a New Era

Leadership in 2025 demands an unprecedented blend of adaptability, emotional intelligence, and technical acumen. As organizations navigate complexities in communication and culture, the path to effective leadership is both a personal journey and a strategic undertaking. In this chapter, we embark on a comprehensive reflection, examining the evolving landscape, the impact of artificial intelligence, and the actionable best practices that define high-performing leaders today.

The Foundations of Modern Leadership

Defining Leadership in 2025

Leadership is no longer confined to traditional hierarchies. The digital revolution, cultural shifts, and global interconnectedness have forged new expectations. Today's leaders are facilitators, visionaries, and catalysts for collaboration.

- Vision: Setting clear goals while remaining agile to change.

- Empathy: Understanding team dynamics and individual aspirations.

- Strategic Communication: Navigating digital channels and fostering authentic dialogue.

Chart: Leadership Styles (2025)

Style	Key Attributes	Adaptability	AI Enablement
Transformational	Inspires, motivates, innovates	High	AI assistants for vision mapping
Servant	Empathy, support, growth focus	Medium	AI for personalized development
Participative	Collaborative, inclusive	High	AI-powered feedback analytics
Transactional	Clear structure, reward-based	Low	AI for task automation

AI and the Future of Leadership

Artificial Intelligence: Friend or Foe?

AI is now an indispensable tool for leaders, enhancing decision-making, automating routine tasks, and enabling deeper insights into organizational trends. However, responsible use is paramount.

- Predictive Analytics: AI can forecast team performance and project outcomes, empowering leaders to make data-driven decisions.

- Natural Language Processing: Tools like chatbots and sentiment analysis streamline communication and measure team morale.

- Talent Management: AI systems help identify strengths and development opportunities, fostering personal growth pathways.

Chart: AI Applications in Leadership

Application	Function	Benefit
Team Analytics	Performance tracking	Real-time feedback, early issue detection
Learning Platforms	Customized skill training	Personalized learning, scalable development

Communication Bots	Automated queries	Improved response time, clarity
Scenario Simulations	Leadership practice	Risk-free environment, accelerated growth

Self-Reflection in Leadership

Why Reflect?

Great leaders dedicate time to self-reflection, assessing strengths, weaknesses, biases, and aspirations. Reflection unlocks growth, offering clarity for decision-making and resilience during uncertainty.

- Regular Journaling: Document leadership challenges and victories.

- Feedback Loops: Encourage 360-degree feedback, leveraging AI tools for objective analysis.

- Peer Review: Share insights with trusted colleagues for a broader perspective.

Best Practice: The Leadership Reflection Framework

Step 1: Define your values and vision.

Step 2: Assess current skills and gaps.

Step 3: Analyze feedback from the team and AI-powered analytics.

Step 4: Set actionable goals for development.

Step 5: Review progress quarterly and iterate.

Communication Challenges and Solutions

Modern Communication Obstacles

From remote work to multicultural teams, communication is fraught with nuance. Leaders must bridge digital divides and ensure clarity.

- Digital Fatigue: Address over-reliance on email and video meetings.

- Cross-cultural Sensitivity: Use AI translators and culture-mapping tools.

- Transparency: Share decisions openly and encourage dialogue.

Chart: Communication Tools for Leaders

Tool	Primary Use	AI Features
Slack	Instant messaging	Sentiment analysis, automated reminders
Zoom	Meetings	AI transcription, meeting highlights
Teams	Collaboration	Project tracking, chatbot assistants

Building and Sustaining Culture

Culture as a Leadership Lever

Culture is a living system shaped by leadership. Strong cultures support innovation, adaptability, and engagement.

- Define Core Values: Use AI surveys to gauge cultural alignment.

- Diversity & Inclusion: AI can surface hidden biases and recommend inclusive language.

- Recognition Systems: Automate peer-to-peer praise to reinforce behaviors.

Best Practice: Culture Blueprint Strategy

Step 1: Articulate mission and values.

Step 2: Map employee experience via data visualization.

Step 3: Identify gaps and implement targeted initiatives.

Step 4: Celebrate wins and iterate.

Collaboration in the Age of AI

Enhancing Teamwork with Technology

Collaboration is supercharged by AI, which facilitates project management, resource allocation, and learning.

- Collaborative Platforms: Integrate AI-powered brainstorming and scheduling tools.

- Knowledge Sharing: Use intelligent repositories for cross-team synergy.

- Conflict Resolution: AI mediation tools surface issues before escalation.

Chart: Collaboration Metrics (Sample Data)

Metric	Pre-AI Era	AI-Enabled
Project Completion Rate	78%	92%
Employee Satisfaction	70%	88%

Cross-team Initiatives	12/year	25/year

Skill Building for Tomorrow's Leaders

Continuous Learning in Leadership

Leaders must continually refresh and expand their skill set. AI-powered platforms offer personalized learning pathways.

- Microlearning: Deliver content in digestible modules.

- Skill Gap Analysis: Use AI to identify and act on development needs.

- Mentorship Matching: Connect mentors and mentees through intelligent algorithms.

Chart: Top Skills for 2025 Leaders

Skill	Importance	AI Training Method
Emotional Intelligence	High	Scenario simulations, feedback analysis
Adaptability	High	Personalized challenges, coaching bots
Digital Literacy	Essential	Interactive tutorials

Best Practices in Leadership Today

Summary of Proven Approaches

- Lead with Empathy: Foster psychological safety and inclusiveness.

- Leverage Technology: Use AI to eliminate inefficiencies and deepen insights.

- Prioritize Well-being: Model work-life balance and resilience.

- Embrace Feedback: Regularly collect and act on data-driven insights.

- Cultivate Diversity: Build teams with varied backgrounds and perspectives.

Case Study: AI-Driven Leadership Transformation

A mid-sized tech company integrated AI analytics into its leadership framework, resulting in a 30% improvement in employee engagement and a 25% reduction in attrition rates over one year. Leaders reported increased confidence in decision-making and greater focus on strategic initiatives.

The Role of Mentorship and Peer Networks

Growing Together

Peer networks and mentorship are vital for sustained growth. AI tools can facilitate matching and monitor progress.

- Network Building: Attend leadership forums and digital communities.

- Knowledge Exchange: Share best practices regularly.

- Mentorship: Set clear goals and track outcomes using digital dashboards.

Conclusion: Charting Your Path Forward

The journey of leadership is a dynamic process of reflection, adaptation, and continual learning. By embracing technology and best practices and by fostering a culture of empathy and inclusion, today's leaders are poised to meet the challenges of tomorrow. As you step into the new year, let these insights guide your evolution, ensuring your leadership leaves a lasting, positive impact.

Chapter 11

The Imperative for Resilient, Servant Leadership

Introduction

In the era of AI disruption, cultural shifts, and unprecedented organizational change, resilience has become the defining skill of leadership. Leaders are no longer measured solely by their ability to execute tasks or meet short-term goals—they are measured by their capacity to inspire, adapt, and sustain teams through volatility.

Resilient leadership combines **inner endurance** with **external agility**, guiding organizations not only to survive but thrive. At the same time, servant leadership—a philosophy rooted in trust, empowerment, and service—provides a timeless framework for developing human-centered organizations where employees flourish, innovation thrives, and values guide decision-making.

This chapter explores how leaders can integrate **resilience, servant leadership principles, and AI-enabled insights** to future-proof their organizations.

Why Resilience Matters

Resilience is no longer optional. Leaders face challenges ranging from AI-driven operational shifts to global crises and rapid cultural transformations. Resilient leaders:

- Inspire trust and confidence
- Sustain performance under pressure
- Enable adaptive responses to uncertainty

Real-World Context:

- **Pandemic recovery** demanded leaders who could balance agility with empathy.

- **AI transformations** require leaders who anticipate change while protecting team morale.

- **DEI challenges** illustrate that adaptability without core values undermines resilience (e.g., Target's DEI program rollback).

Key Insight: McKinsey research shows that leaders who integrate resilience with adaptability are **3–4 times more likely to drive innovation, engagement, and performance**.

Pillars of Resilient Leadership

Resilient leadership can be cultivated through a Mind-Body-Soul framework:

Pillar	Focus	Actionable Strategies	AI/Digital Tools	Outcome
Mind	Cognitive clarity	Mindfulness, Pomodoro breaks	AI focus apps (Focusmate, Notion AI)	Enhanced productivity & attention
Body	Physical well-being	Movement breaks, standing meetings	Wearables, health trackers	Reduced fatigue, increased energy
Soul	Emotional connection	Gratitude exercises, peer recognition	AI feedback tools	Improved morale & team cohesion

Best Practices:

- Reframe challenges as opportunities (Optimism)

- Embrace experimentation (Adaptability)

- Prioritize wellness and stamina (Endurance)

- Align decisions with vision (Purpose)

- Manage stress proactively

- Build strong support networks

Diagram Placeholder: *"Pyramid of Resilience: Mind → Body → Soul → Integrated Leadership Performance"*

Servant Leadership as a Resilience Multiplier

Servant leadership emphasizes **service, empathy, and stewardship**, placing the growth and well-being of others at the heart of leadership. By combining **servant leadership principles with resilience**, leaders create an environment where teams recover faster, innovate more, and sustain high performance.

10 Core Principles of Servant Leadership:

1. Listening

2. Empathy

3. Healing

4. Awareness

5. Persuasion

6. Conceptualization

7. Foresight

8. Stewardship

9. Commitment to the growth of others

10. Building community

Comparative Insight:

Traditional Leadership	Servant Leadership
Authority-focused	Trust-focused
Top-down decisions	Collaborative decisions
Short-term gains	Long-term growth
Power-driven	Service-driven

Diagram Placeholder: *Servant Leadership → Employee Resilience → Organizational Outcomes*

Embedding Resilience Across Teams

Team-level resilience amplifies organizational success. Practices include:

- **Daily micro-check-ins** to gauge team wellbeing

- **Psychological safety**: Encourage risk-taking and idea sharing

- **Adaptive workflows** using agile principles

- **Micro-recognition**: Celebrate incremental wins

AI Integration:

- Sentiment analysis on communication platforms identifies stress early

- Project management AI tools optimize workflows and monitor task completion

Diagram Placeholder: Resilience-Driven Team Cycle: Stress → Adaptive Response → Recovery → Growth

Leading Through AI-Enhanced Disruption

AI is a **force multiplier** for resilient leadership:

- Scenario planning and predictive risk management

- Machine learning to identify operational bottlenecks

- Real-time dashboards for performance, engagement, and stress monitoring

Key Takeaway: Leaders who integrate AI insights with human-centered practices outperform peers in **adaptability, retention, and innovation**.

Chart Placeholder: *Productivity vs. AI Adoption in Leadership Decision-Making*

Measuring Organizational Resilience

Organizational resilience can be tracked and strengthened through key metrics:

- Employee engagement & well-being scores

- Team retention and turnover rates

- Time-to-adapt for projects or crisis responses

- Productivity metrics linked to resilience initiatives

Diagram Placeholder: *Radar Chart: Organizational Resilience Dimensions – Leadership, Team Dynamics, AI Integration, Employee Wellbeing, Agility*

Best Practice: Conduct quarterly resilience audits and leverage AI dashboards for real-time insights.

Case Studies of Resilient Leadership

Leader	Organization	Resilience Practice	Outcome
Jacinda Ardern	New Zealand Govt	Empathetic crisis communication	Public trust & rapid recovery
Satya Nadella	Microsoft	Cultural transformation & cloud pivot	Renewed growth & innovation

Indra Nooyi	PepsiCo	Inclusive leadership & long-term strategy	Strong performance & employee loyalty

Insight: Resilient leaders combine **emotional intelligence, adaptability, and strategic vision**, turning disruption into opportunity.

Key Takeaways for Leaders

1. Resilience is learnable, measurable, and scalable

2. Servant leadership underpins team and organizational well-being

3. AI accelerates resilience but cannot replace empathy and vision

4. Embedding resilience across culture and systems ensures organizational longevity

5. Leaders thrive not in spite of disruption, but because of it

Conclusion

This chapter commenced with a thorough exploration of the concept of resilient leadership, emphasizing the integration of complementary attributes within a servant leadership paradigm. The discourse addressed best practices and highlighted the ways in which servant leadership functions as a catalyst for resilience, referencing a variety of illustrative charts and key takeaways to solidify these insights. The importance of inspiring both internal and external stakeholders was underscored as fundamental to the advancement of a servant leadership organization.

As the journey to becoming effective servant leaders continues, the necessity of cultivating resilience alongside a commitment to mentorship, coaching, and sponsorship was stressed. Through these collaborative efforts, individuals are collectively encouraged to strive for personal and professional growth. By sharing unique, innate talents with families, colleagues, and the wider community, leaders contribute to a culture of support and development that extends far beyond organizational boundaries.

"Do not judge me by my successes; judge me by how many times I fell and got back up again."

– Nelson Mandela

Book Summary
A Guide to Leadership in a Transforming World

In a time characterized by relentless digital transformation, leadership stands at a critical crossroads—requiring bold vision, adaptability, and authenticity. This book serves as both a scholarly resource and a pragmatic toolkit, drawing from the wisdom of elite academic institutions and leading consulting firms, such as MIT Sloan, Harvard, McKinsey, Deloitte, and Gartner. Through a blend of rigorous research, hands-on case studies, and practical recommendations, the book illuminates the rapidly evolving landscape of organizational leadership and the skills needed to thrive within it.

Readers are invited to explore multifaceted challenges and dynamic opportunities that confront leaders in the digital age. Central themes include the indispensable value of emotional intelligence in building resilient, empathetic teams; the promise and complexities of artificial intelligence reshaping the future of work; and strategies for navigating digital transformation with agility and foresight. Each chapter presents actionable frameworks, reflective exercises, and real-world examples, bridging theory to practice and empowering leaders at every stage of their journey.

The book distills vital lessons from global thought leaders: the necessity of lifelong learning, the power of empathetic communication, and the strategic advantage of inclusive leadership. Technology emerges as both a catalyst for innovation and a challenge requiring operational excellence. The narrative emphasizes the importance of adaptability and the courage to embrace complexity and ambiguity, especially within high-stakes environments.

Ultimately, this guide challenges its readers to chart their own course—driven by insight, grounded in purpose, and committed to creating lasting impact. It equips aspiring and current leaders alike with the tools and wisdom to reflect, adapt, and prosper, shaping organizations where people and ideas flourish in a rapidly transforming world.

Book References

- Accenture. (n.d.). *Technology vision: Innovation for a post-digital world.*

- Akinpelu, A. (2024). Transformational leadership: The how and why. *Forbes.*

- Articles from Harvard Business Review on Leadership, Collaboration and Teams, and Inclusion.

- Bain & Company. (2018). *Results delivery: Busting three common myths of change management.*

- Bain & Company. (n.d.). *The journey to agile leadership.*

- Bass, B. M. (1985). *Leadership and performance beyond expectations.*

- Bersin by Deloitte, "HR Technology Market 2024"

- Bersin by Deloitte. (2024). *HR technology market 2024.*

- Bersin, J., & Chamorro-Premuzic, T. (2019). The rise of the inclusive leader. *Deloitte Review.*

- Blue Rock Search Thought Leadership

- Blue Rock Search. (n d.). Thought leadership.

- Burns, J. M. (1978). *Leadership.*

- Coca-Cola Organizational Culture. (2024). Panmore Institute.

- Deloitte Digital. (2022). *Future of work reports.*

- Deloitte Insights (2022). The Role of AI in Employee Empowerment.

- Deloitte Insights: Leadership Trends for 2025.

- Deloitte. (2025). *Investment management outlook.*

- Deloitte. (n.d.). Embracing disruption: Leadership strategies for transformation.

- Diversity Best Practices. (n.d.). Building inclusive leadership for a changing world.

- Dunlop, A. (2021). *Elevating the human experience: Three paths to love and worth at work.*

- Dunlop, A., & Hatfield, S. (2022). *The four factors of trust: How organizations can earn lifelong loyalty.*

- Edmondson, A. (1999). Psychological safety and learning behavior in work teams. *Administrative Science Quarterly, 44*(2), 350–383.

- Edmondson, A. (2018). *The fearless organization.*

- Edmondson, A. (2019). *The fearless organization: Creating psychological safety in the workplace for learning, innovation, and growth.* Wiley.

- Forbes Insights. (n.d.). Leadership in the digital age: A study of business leaders and transformation.

- Forbes, Ad Age, PRWeek, Insider, Money.com. (n.d.). Selected thought leadership articles.

- Gallup (2024). The State of the Global Workplace Report

- Gallup, "State of the Global Workplace"

- Gallup. (2023). *State of the global workplace 2023.*

- Gallup. (2024). *The state of the global workplace report.*

- Gallup. (n.d.). State of the global workplace. Gallup Press.

- Gartner, "Top 5 Trends for the Future of Work"

- Gartner. (n.d.). AI-enabled workforce: Trends and recommendations.

- Gartner. (n.d.). Future of work: AI and workforce evolution.

- Gartner. (n.d.). Top 5 trends for the future of work.

- Gartner: AI-Enabled Workforce: Trends and Recommendations

- GE: Susan Peters on Employee Experience

- Goleman, D. (1995). *Emotional intelligence: Why it can matter more than IQ.* Bantam Books.

- Goleman, D. (2018). Emotional intelligence and leadership effectiveness.

- Google People Analytics Research Portal

- Google. (n.d.). People analytics research portal.

- Grant, A. (2013). *Give and take: Why helping others drives our success.* Penguin Books.

- Greenleaf, R. K. (1977). *Servant leadership: A journey into the nature of legitimate power and greatness.*

- Harvard Business Review (2024). Leading Through AI-Driven Disruption

- Harvard Business Review, "How AI Is Transforming the Workplace"

- Harvard Business Review, (June 2022). "The Era of Bottom-Up Leadership."

- Harvard Business Review. (2018). The real reason people won't change.

- Harvard Business Review. (2022, June). The era of bottom-up leadership.

- Harvard Business Review. (n.d.). Articles on leadership, collaboration and teams, and inclusion.

- Harvard Business Review. (n.d.). How AI is transforming the workplace.

- Harvard Business Review. (n.d.). Leading with emotional intelligence.

- Harvard Business Review: Leading with Emotional Intelligence

- Harvard Business School Online. (n.d.). Digital transformation and leadership.

- Harvard Business School Online: Digital Transformation and Leadership

- Hill, L. A., Brandeau, G., Truelove, E., & Lineback, K. (2014). *Collective genius: The art and practice of leading innovation.* Harvard Business Review Press.

- Hoffman, J. (2023). Leadership is more than a position.

- International Journal of Environmental Research and Public Health. (2023). Career fulfillment and value alignment.

- Jacob Morgan, "The Employee Experience Advantage"

- Kotter, J. (1996). *Leading change.*

- Kotter, J. (2012). *Leading change.* Harvard Business School Press.

- Kotter, J. P. (2012). *Leading change.* Harvard Business Review Press.

- Leinwand, P., & Mainardi, C. (2016). *Strategy that works: How winning companies close the strategy-to-execution gap.* Harvard Business Review Press.

- Leinwand, P., & Mani, M. M. (2021). *Beyond digital: How great leaders transform their organizations and shape the future.* Harvard Business Review Press.

- Liu, Y., Fang, Y., Hu, L. et al. (2024). Inclusive leadership and employee workplace well-being: the role of vigor and supervisor developmental feedback. BMC Psychol 12, 540.

- Liu, Y., Fang, Y., Hu, L., et al. (2024). Inclusive leadership and employee workplace well-being: The role of vigor and supervisor developmental feedback. *BMC Psychology, 12*, 540.

- Maddi, S., & Khoshaba, D. (2024). *Resilience at work.*

- Martin, G. (2025). Resilience: The most coveted leadership skill for 2025. *Forbes.*

- Maxwell, J. C. (2020). Leadership as influence.

- McKinsey & Company (2023). Talent Analytics in Leadership Development.

- McKinsey & Company (2024). Developing a Resilient, Adaptable Workforce for an Uncertain Future

- McKinsey & Company, "Building the Workforce of the Future"

- McKinsey & Company, "Hybrid Work: Making It Fit with Your Diversity, Equity, and Inclusion Strategy"

- McKinsey & Company. (2018). Unlocking success in digital transformations.

- McKinsey & Company. (2023). Talent analytics in leadership development.

- McKinsey & Company. (2024). Developing a resilient, adaptable workforce for an uncertain future.

- McKinsey & Company. (n.d.). Building the workforce of the future.

- McKinsey & Company. (n.d.). Hybrid work: Making it fit with your diversity, equity, and inclusion strategy.

- McKinsey & Company. (n.d.). Leading in the digital era: Case studies and insights.

- McKinsey & Company. (n.d.). The future of leadership— AI and human potential.

- McKinsey & Company: The Future of Leadership—AI and Human Potential

- Mike Walsh. (2025). CEO of Tomorrow—Keynote Address.

- MIT Sloan Management Review. (n.d.). Leadership in the digital era.

- MIT Sloan School of Management. (n.d.). Research on organizational leadership and digital innovation.

- Morgan, J. (2017). *The employee experience advantage.* Wiley.

- Northouse, P. G. (n.d.). *Leadership: Theory and practice.*

- OECD (2021). AI and the Future of Leadership.

- OECD. (2021). AI and the future of leadership.

- Pankowski, M. (2021). *Engaging Gen Z: Lessons to effectively engage Generation Z via marketing, social media, retail, work, and school.*

- Perceptyx. (n.d.). People Insights Platform.

- Perceptyx. People Insights Platform.

- Peter G. Northouse, Leadership: Theory and Practice

- Peters, S. (n.d.). GE: Employee experience. General Electric.

- Prosci. (2022). *Best practices in change management.*

- Raghuram, S., Hill, N. S., Gibbs, J. L., & Maruping, L. M. (2019). Virtual work: Bridging research and practice. *Academy of Management Annals, 13*(1), 285–320.

- Randel, A. E., Dean, M. A., Ehrhart, K. H., et al. (2018). Inclusive leadership: Realizing positive outcomes through belongingness and being valued for uniqueness. *Human Resource Management Review, 28*(2), 190–203.

- Rock, D., Grant, H., & Grey, J. (2016). Diverse teams feel less comfortable — and that's why they perform better. *Harvard Business Review*.

- Salesforce Annual Stakeholder Report (2024)

- Sanborn, M. (2024). Leadership and the meaning of titles.

- Schein, E. H. (2010). *Organizational culture and leadership*. Jossey-Bass.

- Senge, P. M. (1990). *The fifth discipline: The art & practice of the learning organization*. Doubleday.

- Sheppard, B. (2020). *Ten years to midnight: Four urgent global crises and their strategic solutions*. Berrett-Koehler.

- Shore, L. M., Cleveland, J. N., & Sanchez, D. (2018). Inclusive workplaces: A review and model. *Human Resource Management Review, 28*(2), 176–189.

- Society for Human Resource Management (SHRM), "Implementing Flexible Work Arrangements"

- Society for Human Resource Management (SHRM). (2025). Talent Conference Proceedings

- Society for Human Resource Management. (2025). Talent 2025 conference proceedings.

- Society for Human Resource Management. (n.d.). Implementing flexible work arrangements.

- Stellar Leadership: Igniting Excellence Beyond the C-Suite 123.

- Unilever Learning and Development Annual Report. (2024)

- Unilever. (2024). Learning and development annual report.

- United Overseas Bank HR Strategy Case Study

- United Overseas Bank. (n.d.). HR strategy case study.

- Vantage Circle. (2025). Why leaders encourage transformational leadership in 2025?

- Vector Solutions Leadership Insights

- Vector Solutions. (n.d.). Leadership insights.

- Walsh, M. (2025). CEO of Tomorrow—Keynote address.

- Wilkinson, A. D., & Rennaker, M. (2022). The relationship between servant leadership and employee resilience.

- Wojnicki, A. (2024). Demonstrating leadership beyond job titles.

- World Economic Forum (2022). Future of Work and Leadership.

- World Economic Forum, "The Future of Jobs Report 2023"

- World Economic Forum. (2020). *The future of jobs report 2020.*

- World Economic Forum. (2022). Future of work and leadership.

- World Economic Forum. (2023). *The future of jobs report.*

- World Economic Forum. (n.d.). The future of jobs report.

- Zhu, J., & Li, J. (2021). Artificial intelligence in human resource management: Implications for inclusive leadership. *Journal of Business Ethics, 169*(2), 337–352.

The Author

An Excerpt from a University Colloquium Presentation to Doctorial Students

As I reflect over the course of my life and career, there were several turning points—moments of decision, risk, and perseverance that shaped my journey. You have had them as well—the moments that keep you awake at night, or cause you to forget lunch because the decision at hand is so great. I've chosen three of those moments to share with you today.

Turning Point One – Foundations of Resilience

At age 15, I moved from my childhood home in Upstate New York to North Florida, where I lived under the loving care of my grandparents—both of them well into their seventies and eighties.

Life there demanded responsibility. There were nine of us in the household, sometimes as many as 17. Each Thursday, it was my turn to cook, with groceries often running low. I learned to plan, improvise, and reach out to family members to gather what was missing. At first, I couldn't cook at all—my greens and beans barely simmered 15 minutes before I declared them "done." But eyes of wisdom surrounded me, guiding me until I learned.

I hated waiting for that long, bumpy school bus ride that often made us miss breakfast—the most important meal of the day. I worked in the tobacco fields and picked berries and plums to sell in the community. These weren't just chores. They were lessons in **teamwork, survival, creativity**, and **faith**—skills that would carry me into leadership at the highest levels of health care and education.

My mother, a single parent raising five children, was the only one of her 12 siblings to attend college. She was determined that I, her firstborn, would inherit not only her love for education but also her grit. I applied to just one school—her alma mater—and was accepted. My world was small then, but my foundation was rich. Those experiences remain my compass today.

I invite you to reflect on your own foundations. What lessons from your family or community have prepared you for this moment? These are the treasures that will guide you forward.

Turning Point Two – Seizing Bold Opportunities

In 1989, I applied for the New York State Department of Health Fellowship—a nationally competitive program with hundreds of applicants. To my surprise and delight, I was one of only five selected—and the only candidate from out of state.

It was a one-year fellowship with no promise of a job afterward. The risk was real. Yet, it was the **pivotal stepping stone** in my career. I immersed myself in health policy, budget hearings, legislative sessions, and statewide wellness initiatives. I networked with executives across disciplines and discovered that health care isn't an isolated field—it is connected to education, technology, engineering, finance, social services, and beyond.

That fellowship taught me persistence, courage, and the importance of surrounding yourself with **positive people**. It confirmed for me that leadership is about determination, risk-taking, and perseverance.

Turning Point Three – Lifelong Learning

After marriage and returning to Atlanta, I knew I wanted more education. My academic timeline shows both speed and pause:

- **B.S. in 1979**
- **M.S. in 1983**
- **Doctorate in Business Administration, 2002,**
with an advanced graduate certificate in International Business

Nineteen years separated my master's from my doctorate. But education, like life, is a continuous process. I embraced it while balancing career, family, and community. Over the years, my career has allowed me to:

- Serve as a **transformational executive in health care management and higher education**
- Receive **awards and recognition for leadership, innovation, and community service**
- Mentor the next generation of leaders across industries

And I stand before you today because I believe every degree, every milestone, and every detour contributes to the greater journey of **lifelong learning and impact.**

The Author's Message to the Graduates at a University Commencement Ceremony

Look at the person on your right, then on your left, and say together: *"We made it."*

As you prepare to spread your wings, remember:

- Build a circle of positive people.
- Network intentionally.
- Never let others define who you are.
- Be bold, be creative, and be influential.

Your University or college has given you not only knowledge, but also validation of your dreams. You are now the advocates and ambassadors of your great institution.

Your future is bright—think globally, act boldly, and carry forward the spirit of service and leadership.

And I leave you with words paraphrased from Steve Jobs: *"Your time is limited, so don't waste it living someone else's life. Have the courage to follow your heart and intuition."*

Congratulations, Graduates. **You have made it!**

About the Author

Avis D. Dickey, D.B.A., M.S., is a visionary executive, global thought leader, and retired U.S. Navy Reserve Officer with more than 35 years of distinguished leadership across government, health care, education, and the military. A Career Appointed **Senior Executive Service (SES) leader in the federal government for over two decades**, she has held multiple roles engaging employees globally in human capital and veterans' initiatives—**driving transformational strategies that continue to shape workforce excellence and organizational impact worldwide**.

A recognized authority on leadership, organizational transformation, and workforce development, Dr. Dickey is a **highly sought-after speaker** who has delivered inspiring keynote addresses and served as a **university commencement speaker, conference moderator, and doctoral colloquium presenter** for business and health care students. Her engagements span **national and international conferences, leadership summits, military and community forums**, and **executive coaching and mentoring programs** that empower current and emerging leaders.

Throughout her career, she has shared her expertise through **teaching at the master's and doctoral levels**, serving on **doctoral dissertation committees**, and guiding students and professionals toward excellence in leadership, ethics, and innovation. Her board service includes **executive officer roles and committee leadership**, advancing organizational missions in both the public and private sectors.

A **decorated Navy veteran** with worldwide tours of duty and a recipient of multiple military honors, including two Joint Service Achievement Medals, Dr. Dickey embodies the highest standards of service, discipline, and compassion. She is known for her **passion, empathy, and unwavering commitment to developing others**, and for her ability to **inspire transformation and resilience** in the face of change.

As she expands her global platform with the release of her new leadership book, Dr. Dickey continues to **elevate, empower, and transform the future of executive influence**—building leaders who lead with vision, courage, and heart.